29635

289

990

90
990
991

EB 1992
1992
R 1992

# NOT THE WHOLE TRUTH
## An Autobiography

# Not the Whole Truth

## AN AUTOBIOGRAPHY

## PATRICK LICHFIELD

Constable · London

First published in Great Britain 1986
by Constable and Company Limited
10 Orange Street London WC2H 7EG
Copyright © 1986 Patrick Lichfield
Set in Linotron Ehrhardt 12pt by
Rowland Phototypesetting Limited
Bury St Edmunds, Suffolk
Printed in Great Britain by
St Edmundsbury Press Limited
Bury St Edmunds, Suffolk

British Library CIP data
Lichfield, Patrick
Not the whole truth; an autobiography
1. Lichfield, Patrick   2. Photographers
– Great Britain – Biography
I. Title
770'.92'4   TR140.L5

ISBN 0 09 467390 X

For Rose, Thomas and Eloise,
who might learn a little
from this cautionary tale

# ACKNOWLEDGEMENT

A passage in Chapter Ten describes the difficulties I faced in a vain attempt to take my own photograph. Much of what is written there also applies, with almost uncanny precision, to the challenge of preparing this pen portrait; here, however, the assistance has been provided by Ian Martin, whose patience and general perspicacity have proved as indispensable to this project as they were to *Lichfield on Photography*, on which we collaborated in 1981.

## NOTE ON THE ILLUSTRATIONS

All the photographs in this book come from the personal collection of the author (most of them taken by his assistants Chalky Whyte and Peter Kain), with the exception of the following: the photograph of the author with Marie Helvin was taken by Clayton Howard; the photographs of the author at a Blenheim Palace Ball, at Ascot, of the author with David Bailey and Penelope Tree, and as best-dressed man are from Associated Press Limited; the photograph of the author on a motorbike with others from Camera Press; and the photographs of the author with Allegra Carracciolo and the author at Madame Tussaud's are from Popperfoto.

# [ 1 ]

'Patrick Lichfield', of course, is merely a convenient fiction.

Although I have become, in due course, the Rt. Hon. the 5th Earl of Lichfield, Baron Soberton, Viscount Anson, I was christened Thomas Patrick John Anson; strictly speaking, I should be either Patrick Anson or the Earl of Lichfield. But my hybrid pseudonym, casually assumed at an early age, seems to have stuck; only the Press find it insufficient, preferring to dub me, tediously enough, 'Royal-lensman-Lichfield-cousin-of-the-Queen'.

The fairy-tale story that label implies, a renegade royal who swapped his coronet for a camera, is (like most fairy stories) deeply romantic and utterly untrue. Apart from anything else, I'm not strictly the Queen's cousin; I'm merely one of her many first-cousins-once-removed. Her Majesty and I have but one set of great-grandparents in common: the Earl and Countess of Strathmore. One of their ten children, Elizabeth Bowes-Lyon, married the man who became King George VI and had two daughters, now the Queen and Princess Margaret. Elizabeth's brother, John Bowes-Lyon, also had two daughters: my aunt, Diana, and my mother, Anne.

My great-grandmother, the old Countess, died only shortly before I was born and, although I never knew her, the portrait that hung in the castle made her look distinctly formidable; her husband, still very much alive throughout my childhood, was an imposing yet kindly man with a big beard which regularly caught fire whenever he lit a cigarette. Officially he was the 14th

Earl of Strathmore and Kinghorne, Viscount Lyon and Baron Glamis, Tannadyce, Sidlaw and Strathdichtie, Baron Bowes, of Streatlam Castle, County Durham and Lunedale, County York. We called him Big Grandpa.

His son, the aforementioned John (usually known as Jock) married a wonderful Irishwoman with an equally wonderful name: Fenella Hepburn Stuart-Forbes-Trefusis. She was a magically dotty woman who was, perhaps unsurprisingly, fascinated by names in general and nicknames in particular; her cousin Sidney Elphinstone, for example, a deeply serious amateur photographer who disappeared for hours beneath the black curtain of his huge plate camera, was always known as Uncle Tortoise. On one occasion she gave a rather grand cocktail party for over a hundred people which was notable for the fact that none of the guests seemed in any way connected; the new Mrs Lyon, fascinated by her surname, had simply combed the telephone book for others in a similar position: Sir Eric Partridge, Lady Bird, Quentin Hogg, Michael Swann, Doris Hare, Cyril Stagge, Michael Leach . . .

The Lyons have been Thanes of Glamis for hundreds of years, custodians of a huge and attractively sinister castle festooned with battlemented turrets and riddled with hidden rooms and secret passageways, the repository of a long and crowded history that includes a private hangman, a standing army, much bloodshed and numerous scandals.

It also had ghosts like other places have mice. We shared our accommodation with a famous but largely unseen host of phantasmagorical figures, including The Tongueless Woman, The Black Boy, Earl Beardie and Jack the Runner. The most reliable of them all, and the least disturbing, was The Grey Lady, who could occasionally be found at prayer in the ornate castle chapel. In my mother's day seeking her out became such an after-dinner ritual that my great-grandfather rearranged the pews in an attempt to dislodge her; she remained, however, still praying in the middle of a pew. (The chapel is also noted for its picture of Christ in a hat, a sartorial detail added by the artist in a fit of pique when he discovered that the doors would not be unlocked until he'd painted the ceiling as well as the walls.)

Where other houses had drawing-rooms, sitting-rooms and studies, Glamis had The Hangman's Chamber, The Crypt and, spookiest of all, The Room of Skulls, where the Lord of Glamis once reluctantly agreed to hide a party of renegade Ogilvies. He hid them all too well, apparently; they were only discovered several centuries later, a pile of bleached bones locked behind a very solid door.

The Strathmores seem to have had a fondness for locked rooms; the one story which we were never, ever, allowed to talk about concerned a strange forebear who'd been kept hidden in a secret room somewhere deep in the Castle, silently growing to an immense age in total obscurity. Much more visible were Glamis' guests, a constant flow of friends and relations all of whom seemed to me to be incredibly old. I escaped their well-meaning but sometimes over-critical attentions with visits to the Wishing Well, where everything I asked for (including a pet ferret) seemed to come true.

Glamis was a magical, liberating place and I wish I could have spent more of my childhood there. Regrettably, we were only visiting.

I was born in my grandmother's house in Embankment Gardens, London W. on 25th April 1939. Some six weeks earlier Neville Chamberlain assured the country that the outlook in international affairs was 'tranquil'; some four months later he changed his mind and declared we were at war. My father, a professional soldier, more or less disappeared for the duration on service overseas.

The war, for a small child at least, was exciting rather than

[ 9 ]

threatening, a mysterious time in which anything could and did happen, including the overnight transformation of the hundreds of trees in Windsor's Long Walk into a forest of silver foil. (Disillusioned with age, I now realise that those huge drifts of airborne tinsel were designed to jam our defensive radar.)

For a while, we lived close to Windsor Castle, where my sister and I were once taken to see a performance of *Aladdin* whose cast included the teen-aged Princesses Elizabeth and Margaret. The Castle was also the place for dancing lessons with an extraordinarily flamboyant old duck called Madame Marguerite Vacani, whose speciality was the polka. The polka has always struck me as a singularly pointless exercise but Mme Vacani had taught it to all the Royal Family and would surely have taught it to us too, had we stopped at Windsor long enough. Again, though, we were only passing through.

My memory is of a childhood spent in constant motion, commuting from one end of the country to the other like demented lost luggage, staying with grandparents, great-grandparents, and what seemed like hundreds of aunts, uncles, great-aunts and great-uncles scattered like grapeshot across the kingdom. Never having known differently I assumed that this was the way all families lived, just as I assumed all nannies went to bed with their boots on in case there was an air raid in the middle of the night.

In London we rested briefly at my maternal grandmother's house in Charles Street, conveniently located close to the American Servicemen's Club in Grosvenor Square, outside which my sister Elizabeth could usually be found standing like an infant streetwalker soliciting supplies of rare wartime chocolates. Mme Vacani, whom I suspected of following us, also turned up in London and the dancing lessons continued, palliated somewhat by visits afterwards to Gunther's Tea Rooms in Park

Lane (on a site that was later to house, somewhat ironically, Hugh Hefner's Playboy Club).

A friend of mine was in Gunther's one day towards the end of the war when an air raid began. As the sedate atmosphere was increasingly disrupted by the sound of explosions coming closer and closer the waiters disappeared beneath the table-cloths, leaving the nannies and their charges to display character-istically British phlegm as the plaster dust sifted down on to their meringues and *milles feuilles*. Finally, with a massive crump, a bomb destroyed the house next door; the windows blew in, the lights went out and part of the ceiling collapsed. 'What was that, Nanny?' asked my friend. 'It's a bomb, dear,' she replied. 'Elbows off the table.'

We had our own bomb in Charles Street, an incendiary device that landed in my mother's freshly run bath. Liz and I were beside ourselves with excitement; my mother less so and we left for the safety of the countryside the next morning. On my mother's side of the family there was not only Big Grandpa at Glamis, but also the Clintons who had one estate at Heanton in Devon and another at Fettercairn in Scotland. My father's parents, the Lichfields, lived in Staffordshire, distinctly isolated in a huge house set in a vast park: Shugborough.

Shugborough turned out to be very safe indeed, despite my grandfather's conviction to the contrary. Equipped with a piercing whistle, he would regularly order us down to hide in the cellars, where the accommodation was strictly ordered according to rank. My grandfather went in with the port; Nanny and I went in with the third footman, the soda-maker and the Rose's Lime Juice. I sat there, with my head between my knees, praying for just a little excitement; a bomb or two to start with, ideally, followed by a small invasion.

It seemed unlikely; the village which gives the house its name, Shugborough, lies long-buried beneath the artful landscape;

Lichfield, a distinctly peaceful city at the best of times, was miles away; Coventry, the nearest real military target, was even further. The only potential target of even remote significance nearby was the railway, the London, Midland and Scottish line that bores through one corner of the estate and which had originally provided the house with its own station. (This facility was sorely missed by my grandfather when it was closed at the beginning of the war but he soon found an answer: pulling the communication cord at just the right moment he would regally hand the guard a five pound note to cover the fine before descending for a short stroll home across the park. Years afterwards, late for a tenants' meeting, I nerved myself to do the same thing only to disappear into a six-foot snowdrift.)

My grandfather took his duties as head of the local Home Guard extremely seriously and he and his brother-in-law spent several hours each day guarding the railway tunnel against the Hun, refreshed at regular intervals by a footman on a bicycle bearing plum cake and Madeira. I was puzzled that these military manoeuvres seemed to be an entirely daylight affair but when I asked what happened at night I was told not to be so stupid: 'Even the Germans wouldn't invade at night.' They showed precious little sign of coming by day either. We had one moment of excitement when a gamekeeper was reported to be holding an airman captive halfway up a tree on account of his suspicious accent; he turned out to be Canadian.

Shugborough's isolation made it frustratingly safe; it also made it very lonely. Outside civilisation was represented, then as now, by the tiny village of Great Haywood, sitting at the edge of the park across the river and definitely out of bounds to me except for the once a week visit when I was allowed to spend my pocket money on a choc-ice at the village post office under Nanny's watchful eye.

The only other dealings I had with the outside world were on

Sundays when we made our ritual visit to church, using the private road that carefully skirted the village. Quite recently I received a letter from a 74-year-old widow who described the scene just after the First World War:

> Every Sunday morning we would walk down to the Essex Bridge and wait to see Lord and Lady Lichfield with their children. We were instructed to curtsey and wish them good morning. The highlight of our day was when her ladyship enquired if we were enjoying our holiday. Lord Lichfield was of a military stature, Lady Lichfield small, petite and beautiful, which made my mother exclaim, "She is just like a piece of Dredsen China."
> Now for my question: Where do you fit into all this?

If my correspondent had returned to the Essex Bridge some twenty-five years later she would have seen me as well, wearing my Sunday suit and bowler hat, being laughed at by the village boys, and asking myself much the same question. I had already worked out that life at Shugborough existed on three very distinct levels: Upstairs, Downstairs and Somewhere In Between. Upstairs, in the big cold rooms, the war had brought on a bout of belt-tightening; no sacrifice was too great, not even the cancellation of our subscription to *The Illustrated London News*.

Downstairs, things were at least a little more lively. An aunt of mine told me that in her day there had been thirty-eight indoor staff plus a similar number working in the grounds; even now, with an entire generation away at war, the house was far from under-staffed. We had, amongst others, our own bee-keeper, our own plumber, our own painter, and our own cabinet maker, each of them fitting into their particular place within a rigidly structured hierarchy. The maids and the footmen lived in a warren of corridors underneath the roof, the chef had his own flat, and Tomlinson, the butler and therefore the head of the hierarchy, had not only his own flat but also his own grand piano. (I was taught to address this paragon as Mister Tomlinson; my grandfather called him Twinkletoes.)

My sister and I existed neither entirely above stairs nor entirely below; we fitted Somewhere In Between, a nebulous zone with shifting borders whose only certainty was The Nursery, a warm, safe place where a fire always burned and a toothache never mattered. In my mother's day, every nursery had had its own entirely separate complement of staff consisting of a Day Nanny, a Night Nanny and several nursery maids; we managed quite happily with just Nanny: Agnes Maxim, a marvellously steadfast East Anglian who'd started as one of my mother's nursery maids (and who later went on to look after my sister's daughter).

She was an eternal comforting presence who remained with us until I was at least sixteen and who became very much the mainstay of my life, standing for no nonsense yet constantly urging us on to better things. We still correspond and, maudlin as it may sound, I still miss her.

In the still room, which luckily enough seemed to have escaped the cuts elsewhere, Mary and Martha provided a constant source of jams, biscuits and ginger-beer and I rapidly established the place as my rainy-day retreat. Another great friend of mine was Fernihough the house carpenter, a highly skilled craftsman whom I watched for hours patiently turning a replacement chair-leg or matching a piece of missing veneer.

Rose, the chauffeur (more of a hero than a friend) impressed me tremendously by the unerring impassivity with which he failed to react to my grandmother's commands, barked at him down the microphone from behind her glass screen. 'Faster, Rose!' she'd snap, or 'Slower, Rose!' and nothing whatsoever would happen. When we sold the Buick in the late fifties we discovered sixteen balls of cotton wool stuffed into the loudspeaker.

I also made friends with the Germans. The house itself had narrowly escaped being commandeered by the Army only to lose a large part of the park to the local authorities, who proceeded to build a huge prisoner-of-war camp for what seemed to be hundreds of aliens. Liz and I had been distinctly short of playthings for most of the war (although Canon Rorrison, the resident chaplain at Glamis, made brilliant paper boats); we now discovered that the Germans carved sensational wooden toys and *Stalag* Shugborough became a regular port of call.

Although I have dim memories of V.J. day celebrations at Windsor, the war ended for me on the day that my father came home from abroad, striding into the Nursery with an armful of what we recognised from our books as bananas. (Amidst all the excitement nobody bothered to tell us to peel them first so we carved them up like apples and ate them skin and all.) My father, for his part, must have known he was well and truly home when, still in his uniform, he was forbidden a second glass of sherry. 'Don't you know there's a war on, old boy?' said my grand-father.

After my father returned, my mother left. Elizabeth and I, accustomed by now to the swings-and-roundabouts theory of Fate, continued to assume this was how all families worked. The next time I saw my mother at Shugborough was to be the last time she visited the house for more than twenty years. Unable to contain my impatience, I had bicycled up to the main grid to wait for her but when she emerged from the car she looked terribly beautiful and terribly tense and little or nothing was said before she climbed back into the Buick and carried on up the drive with me bicycling wildly along in front of her.

Gradually as the weekend passed, I realised something had gone terribly wrong.

I will probably never know what happened between them but the story, I suspect, was far from uncommon: two people, scarcely out of adolescence, meeting, falling in love, marrying, and then, almost immediately, being parted by the war. Five years later, when they were reunited, they'd become different people. The divorce was finalised in 1948 and at Shugborough my mother's name was never mentioned again; at Charles Street, at Glamis, at Heanton and at Fettercairn it was my father who became the non-person. My sister and I learnt, earlier than most, that there are some things of which one simply does not speak.

I imagine it was Nanny who eventually explained things to us but all I really remember is the growing apprehension that I now had yet another home to visit. I was also somewhat distracted by the news that I would shortly begin attending a preparatory school.

What worried me most was not so much the thought of being away from home (wherever that was) as the realisation that I would now be required to mix with large numbers of young boys. My social circle, such as it was, had hitherto been drawn entirely from adults at least twenty to thirty years older than I, and the prospect of having to adapt to my own age group filled me with distinct alarm.

Wellesley House, it transpired, was not only surrounded by the rusting remains of wartime coastal defences but also hard by the original Thirty-Nine Steps, a potent combination of imagery for a fertile young imagination, and the years I spent there proved neither particularly alarming nor excessively threatening but merely dull; boredom alternated with loneliness with occasional eruptions of excitement and a few Major Discoveries.

I discovered, for instance, that I had a relatively good soprano voice which led to my first appearance onstage, singing (or rather not singing, since I forgot the words entirely) 'Who is Sylvia?'

I discovered I could be good at boxing, that I quite liked cricket and rugger, and that I distinctly disliked football.

And, slowly but surely, I discovered how to relate to other boys. 'Swapping' was one of the many crazes that swept the school and I managed, somehow, to talk a classmate into exchanging his wonderful gold-edged crocodile-skin Asprey wallet for a pair of terrier-trimmed tin cufflinks, a shameful trade that eventually came to light during the holidays, producing a series of embarrassed parental telephone calls that culminated in a meeting at St James's Palace to restore the *status quo*. (The boy's father was Sir Michael Adeane, the Private Secretary to the Queen; the boy himself grew up to become the Hon. Edward Adeane, Private Secretary to the Prince of Wales.)

I also discovered that I was not one of nature's academics. English was the only subject in which I was even half-way competent; an accomplishment which had less to do with natural aptitude than with the fact that the man who taught us had honorary hero status as an ex-county-cricketer. (He is now the cricket correspondent of *The Sunday Times*.)

In the holidays, we continued our peripatetic progress, alternating visits to my mother's family with lengthier sojourns at Shugborough, the latter always providing the setting for the thrice-yearly ceremony of the Reading of the School Report. On an empty Sunday afternoon, my grandfather would request my presence in his study where I would find him ensconced behind a vast acreage of desk preparing for an interrogation that resembled nothing so much as the Victorian genre painting, 'When Did You Last See Your Father?' My father, in fact, was to be seen hovering at my grandfather's shoulder, wincing occasionally at a particularly poor mark or scathing comment:

'By the time Anson learns French he will be too old to cross the Channel.'

My grandfather, like the Edwardian he was, cared little for book-learning and concentrated his attention on my sporting performance in general and my shooting in particular. He himself managed to get out with a gun almost every day, the sole exception being Sundays, an iron rule known even to the pheasants, one of which invariably followed us to church once a week, hopping cheerfully alongside him through the park provoking a string of muttered and most un-Christian imprecations. My great-uncle's speciality was shooting pigeons, a faintly ludicrous occupation which he took extremely seriously, daubing his face with thick camouflage paint, laboriously dressing up as a tree and then ponderously ascending the specially constructed rope ladder that led to his hide. Liz and I used to watch these preparations with great solemnity, secure in the knowledge that the cascara we had put in his porridge at breakfast would soon necessitate a somewhat speedier descent.

Although I hated every minute of the two-year apprenticeship I served as a beater, being much too small to keep up, my opinion of shooting improved substantially when I was given my first air-gun, followed by a .22 with which I frightened a great many rooks. I was later allowed to attend the more formal shoots, carrying an unloaded gun, adopting sportsmanlike poses but otherwise keeping well out of the way. I began to spend most of my holidays out and about on various estates, stalking unsuspecting birds under the watchful eye of an assortment of wise old gamekeepers, chief amongst whom was Courtenay who taught me, I think, virtually everything I know about the countryside, and particularly those bits of it which can be shot at with impunity.

My knowledge of safety procedures, the setting of snares and so forth was the subject of close scrutiny from my grandfather and the polish on my boots and the shine on my brasses were always rigorously inspected before I set off to spend the morning crawling through dirt on my elbows.

My indoor education was equally efficient, if somewhat eccentric by today's standards. My sister and I had been eating downstairs with the staff since I was seven and we now began to understudy them, traipsing around learning how to polish china, silver and glass, how to lay fires, and how to iron tablecloths. My sister's years of instruction at various housemaids' knees later proved extremely useful when she began Party Planners; for my part, I learnt that a newspaper briefly placed in a hot oven sheds less ink on the hands.

In the evenings we learnt to wait at table in the servants' hall. Years later, when dining alone one evening with my widowed grandfather he dismissed the butler as he made to serve the port, gruffly saying, 'Let the boy do it.' There hadn't been much call for port in the servants' hall and the strongest drink I knew was Kia-Ora Orange Squash so, erring on the side of caution, I made sure I gave the bottle a good shake before I poured it out. My grandfather was equally shaken, and not a little stirred.

My formal education at Shugborough had at one time been placed in the no doubt capable hands of a governess, Miss Fish, a lady of whom I regret to say I recall nothing save that a bat once became entangled in her hair whilst we were supposed to be studying Nature, a subject that, as taught by her, concentrated on both birds and bees whilst steering resolutely clear of The Birds and The Bees. (Although I was by this time vaguely aware that Sex existed, that it was somehow both a Good Thing and a Bad Thing, and that it was vaguely connected with Making Babies, the whole topic was basically a large mystery. But not for long.)

My mother, now settled in London, was taking various odd jobs to make ends meet, the oddest of which was demonstrating refrigerators at the Ideal Home Exhibition where she earnt the unheard-of sum of £19 a week whilst I ate my way through an unheard-of number of Hovis rolls. Mummy now decided to take my worldly education in hand and selected my godfather for the delicate task of instructing me in the mysteries of What was What and (more to the point) What went Where. My godfather is an extremely nice man of whom I'm very fond but even he, I think, would agree that his dedicated career as a life-long bachelor made him particularly unsuitable for the job. We drove round and round Hyde Park Corner in total silence for about half an hour and then went to the Ritz for a slap-up tea, leaving the nasty business where it belonged, still smouldering on the horizon.

It must have been around this time that I was given my first camera, a considerably more curious gift for a small child then than now. I previously had borrowed my grandfather's Box Brownie, slipping it off the hall table, taking a few quick snaps and slipping it back again, leaving him to puzzle out the origin of the resulting pictures of fuzzy cows.

Taking the camera to Tripoli, where my father was posted, I graduated from cows to donkeys, and even condescended to allow Liz into the picture provided she agreed to act as a donkey tether. That worked well until the day eventually came when she was dragged halfway across Libya and had to spend a considerable time in hospital (where I took my first interior shots). She got her own back in short order by betting me that I couldn't eat an entire tree-load of raw figs; I won the bet and spent several days in the same hospital with acute dysentery.

At the end of our stay, as we boarded the Hermes, a small baby voiced its discontent by screaming its head off. I turned to Nanny, with all the haughtiness of an infant autocrat, and drawled, 'Surely somebody can stop her doing that?' Nanny replied, 'That is Lord Oxford's little daughter, Annunziata, and she has as much right to scream as you have to remain silent.'

It was Annunziata Asquith, with whom I subsequently became great friends when she became my star Burberry model.

Back in England, my education continued to develop in unexpected ways. In common with most of my classmates, I studied Unofficial Biology with our games mistress, a woman best referred to in classic euphemistic style as Miss G.

She would appear at the door of our dormitory after lights out to invite selected parties to her room where we would be encouraged to discuss anatomy in general, and her anatomy in particular. Innocent and entirely well-meaning as it was, in retrospect it seems a little too much too soon. If the fruit had remained forbidden, cloaked in reassuring humbug about Respecting One's Partner and so forth, the romantic flame might have successfully smouldered on into adolescence; as it was my teenage sexuality flared briefly and then went out completely, not to be relit for several more years.

Not that there would be much opportunity for it to do otherwise given the nature of my next port of call.

# [ 2 ]

As the time for me to enter Harrow grew steadily closer, my prep school masters grew steadily more embarrassed by the indecorous illustrations of couples on sofas that began to decorate the margins of my homework. Developed by a schoolmaster uncle of mine, holiday-cramming me for the Common Entrance exam, they were designed to illustrate the difference between the Active and the Passive Mode, a distinction which I cared little about at the time but would have great cause to remember in years to come.

This academic preparation, rigorous as it was, paled into utter insignificance beside my grandfather's determined efforts to instil in me what he considered to be an essential working knowledge of the Lore and Legend of Harrow, a hefty but unwritten tome that had been steadily accumulating since John Lyon first endowed the school in 1571. Harrow, it seemed, was strong on Tradition, not least in the vexed matter of the school uniform, a complex and time-honoured dress code that signalled one's precise position on the ladder of achievement by awarding, or withholding, rights (or 'privs') to variously coloured scarves, ties and handkerchiefs.

A coloured ribbon on a straw hat, a button fastened here or unfastened there could, apparently, make all the difference; I struggled through endless summer evenings inserting and removing collar-studs and cuff-links until my fingertips ached and my mind reeled. My least favourite item of all was the inaptly named Eton collar, a stiff, white, starched affair that extended itself half way across the shoulders and which all young boys were expected to wear until they reached the regulation height of 5′2″ and moved on to the equally traditional, and equally uncomfortable, tail-coat and long grey trousers. If (or so far as my grandfather was concerned when) I became a member of a First Eleven or First Fifteen, I would be invited to assume the ultimate 'Blood's Priv', the distinctive grey waistcoat of 'The Phil', an élite within an élite that had long since abandoned its early interest in philately to become a self-perpetuating mutual admiration society for sporty scholars.

I never made it into 'The Phil'; I had more than enough trouble making it into long trousers. My height when I entered Harrow was 4′10″ and it remained so, stubbornly, for at least another two and a half years; my early adolescence was spent striving to grow taller whilst above me a race of supermen, several yards high with broken voices, effortlessly negotiated the labyrinthine subtleties of what I began to realise was not so much an independent school as an independent culture.

I read recently of a new housemaster at Harrow being shown around his quarters by the Head of House, a surprisingly short tour which ended at a green baize door.

'Everything that happens on this side of the door is your responsibility,' said the boy. 'Everything beyond it is mine. When you wish to enter my side of the House you will knock and wait to be invited.'

I'd be tempted to dismiss this story as pure apocrypha were it not that in my House just such a door existed, marking off the housemaster's 'Private Side' where new boys spent their first term in protective custody before being thrust, untimely, into the hothouse world beyond.

Once through that door, it was every boy for himself, and the weakest to the wall. I dreaded it, particularly on the last day of the holidays when the determination not to blub was at its weakest. I even ran away once, realising too late that the real trick is to have something to run to, rather than from. I, having no clear goals, simply hung around London's parks and Underground stations for a day and a half waiting to be discovered by the police to whom I duly unfolded a lengthy and highly polished story about a man who'd invited me home to look at his stamp collection. My return to school was further delayed by a day spent happily travelling around London in a police car consistently just failing to identify my abductor and I rounded things off with a virtuoso imitation of acute appendicitis, a desperate ploy that resulted only in the speedy removal of one very small, very healthy appendix.

My favourite Old Harrovian at the time was Byron and further research revealed that he, far from running away, had once attempted to blow the place up. I settled down to further study. Other old boys included at least half a dozen assorted Prime Ministers, several Kings, Nubar Gulbenkian and, perhaps most curious of all, Cecil Beaton. Each of these luminaries had suffered not so much an education as an indoctrination, living and working under a regime most charitably described as 'character-forming'.

The emphasis on formation of character excused a multitude of sins, not the least of which was the almost incredibly primitive accommodation, a piquant mixture of grandeur and squalor that my grandfather later confirmed had survived unchanged since at least his time and probably longer. Harrow was squalid, grubby and extremely cold, unsurprisingly so, since every bucket of coal had to be dragged up several flights of stairs by hand; although matters had improved slightly since the eighteenth century (when boys wanting a bed to themselves were required to pay a special fee), each boy's room was still little more than a cupboard with a wooden bed and a canvas mattress that had to be let down from the wall at night.

What little individuality we managed to maintain was expressed by the way these rooms were decorated. (I felt my Archibald Thorburn prints of pheasants, woodcock and grouse lent considerable tone, more so perhaps than the guilty delights of the Cyd Charisse pin-ups that I secreted above the bed.)

Beneath the bed was an all purpose wicker receptable that housed damp games clothes, old boots and food parcels from home including, in my case, the Fortnum and Mason game pie that my clever mother sent me and which I, an early entrepreneur, sold off in slices to my hungry co-habitees. In the winter we cooked sooty bangers on the open fires; in the summer we were warmer but considerably more hungry. For the older boys, the culinary climax of the week was the Fines Breakfast, a traditional test of resourcefulness that began when Harrow's early pupils had to find their own Sunday meals, the servants being away in church. By my time the whole business had taken on the dimensions of a bizarre cross between a Scavenger Hunt and the Henley Regatta with various groups vying to outdo the others, a special prestige accruing to anyone clever enough to acquire a pink grapefruit.

In keeping with the empire-building ethos that still clung, tenuously, to Harrow's ivied walls, these meals were not, of course, prepared by the senior boys themselves, but merely planned (and eaten) by them. The actual work, here as everywhere else, was left to the junior boys, the Fags, a terrified under-race who lived with one ear constantly cocked for the long loud summons from on high: 'Boy. Boy! BOOOOOY!!!' Since the last boy to arrive inevitably got the job, a scrum would be forming even before the cry had died, a desperate knot of youthful determination that rolled up four or more flights of stairs, kicking, gouging and punching in a small riot of character formation. The smallest lost, and I found myself supplementing Shugborough's domestic education with an endless round of boot-cleaning, coal-heaving and errand-running, evolving rapidly into the tiniest, best-trained, least-paid manservant in the history of Harrow.

I also found out about beating. The first official beating that I had had, over and above Nanny's ministrations with the back of a hairbrush, was at my prep school; I'd been severely surprised to discover just how low was my threshold for physical discomfort. At Harrow I discovered an entirely new dimension of pain, amplified and extended by a bizarre ritual theatre.

A misdemeanour, once reported, set in motion a system of organised retribution that moved with an impressively awesome lack of pace. The process began with a 'Haul-Up'. The offender would be gravely summoned from the silence of late-night prep to present himself in the Head of House's room where a group of senior boys would lay the facts of the matter before him. Arguments would be heard, statutes cited and excuses shot down in flames before the tribunal retired to deliberate behind closed doors.

This trial by ordeal was quite capable of being prolonged over several haul-ups spread over several weeks until finally judgement was delivered: the offender would be beaten, not today, probably not tomorrow, but certainly at some time in the near future. The waiting began, made no easier by the knowledge that the Head of House was Public Schools' Rackets Champion, the athletic owner of a perfect forehand smash. In time, just as it became quite obvious that the whole thing had surely been forgotten or (even less likely) forgiven, the terrible call would come echoing down the sleeping corridors, summoning the duty fag to summon in turn the miserable miscreant.

The event itself rarely proved anti-climactic; it was not unknown for blood to be drawn and it was rumoured that Matron was ordered to be on stand-by with smelling salts to revive the wounded. At the end of the proceedings all of the parties involved gravely thanked the others before leaving. We were, after all, nothing if not perfect gentlemen.

There was more to life at Harrow than food, fagging and flogging of course; a little teaching was somehow fitted in now and again for instance. But the ultimate jewel in Harrow's cultural crown was neither scholastic, nor sporty, nor sartorial; it was Songs. And, as so often there, my first experience of it was the worst, an obligatory initiation in which each new boy in turn was expected to stand on a table in front of his entire House whilst rendering, utterly unaccompanied and in a voice that was inevitably just about to break, the first verse of 'Men of Harlech'. Once past that hurdle, and after endless rehearsals, we were considered ready for 'House Songs' and, eventually, 'School Songs', choral concerts held each term before a specially invited audience of Old Harrovians, chief amongst whom was usually Sir Winston Churchill.

On the evening that I remember best he was serenaded with all the old favourites from the Harrow Song Book including 'Forty Years On', as immortalised by Alan Bennett, on this occasion retitled 'Sixty Years On' and extended by several verses saluting the patriarch himself. But the song that I remember, and which I am still liable to break into at the slightest encouragement, was one that struck me as somewhat more relevant to my own situation:

Five hundred faces and all so strange!
Life in front of me – home behind,
I felt like a waif before the wind
Tossed on an ocean of shock and change.

As the final notes died away, Churchill could be seen sitting motionless centre stage, the tears streaming down his portly cheeks. He came down from The Hill that night, car and all, on a swiftly improvised raft of planks and beams, carried at shoulder height by cheering schoolboys in a proud gesture of solidarity from one institution to another. I toyed with the possibility of becoming a Prime Minister rather than a rebel poet, took the elementary precaution of putting my name down for boxing lessons, and settled in for the long slow march towards manhood.

My companions included not only boys from other countries but also from other classes, the State Assisted Scholars that we patronised half to death with endless explanations of the finer points of pheasant shooting. Not that there were many State Scholars in my house; Elmfield, where my father, grandfather and great-grandfather had been before me, was unashamedly aristocratic in tone if not in accommodation. It was also distinctly competitive.

Willy Fox, later known to the world as James, had a definite head start thanks to his early child-star role in *The Magnet*. Glen McCorquodale's athletic prowess won him similar hero status, only slightly dented by the discovery that his mother wrote romantic novels and called herself Barbara Cartland; Lance Callingham's mother, on the other hand, Lady Docker, dealt his reputation an almost irretrievable blow by arriving in a Daimler with gold spots on it.

One of Harrow's more genteel customs was that boys in their last term distributed photographs of themselves to a select list of those who were left behind. As these tokens of a life beyond the walls spread all too slowly around my room, I realised that my relatively unique position as one of only four or five camera-owners in the school could be converted into sorely needed hard cash. Further research revealed that the photographs were taken by Hill and Saunders who used a huge and extremely formal plate camera at half a crown a shot. I, using my extremely informal Kodak Retinette, did it for ninepence.

The money, when added to the savings made by not putting stamps on my infrequent letters to my father, allowed me to extend my equipment to include an exposure meter and a tiny flash gun; my room gained, as an added decorative motif, a crunching carpet of used blue bulbs as I transferred my photographic allegiance from cows to stopped-action ping-pong balls. My camera accompanied me everywhere, particularly to sports fixtures, where I took great delight in capturing the McCorquodale brothers' discomfiture as their mother spoon fed them with Royal Jelly. And when I discovered that every film handed over every counter of every Boots the Chemist came straight to Harrow for processing, I swiftly made some new friends and spent hours processing prints in West Street.

The school play, *King Lear*, provided further photographic opportunities, although my experiments with ping-pong balls proved sadly inadequate to the task of freezing the flight of Gloucester's plucked-out eyeballs, a pair of peeled grapes that hit the stage with a stomach-turning squish. Gruesome props such as these were the hallmarks of my House Master, Ronald Watkins, a Shakespearian scholar with an international reputation who always directed the school play and always managed a first-night smile when presented with a signed copy of the latest Barbara Cartland opus.

A year later when, despite endless rehearsals in the privacy of my room, I failed to capture Hollywood interest for my cameo role as Third, or possibly Fourth, Roman Citizen (sole line as I recall: 'Burn, burn, burn') I decided to be a test match cricketer rather than a film star and cajoled my way into the under-sixteen team chosen to play Eton away. At the tea-interval, hearing that the Queen was there inspecting the cadet force, I rushed off to take what would have been my first Royal pictures, had an officious cadet not ripped the film from my camera.

Though strong, I was still quite small, a slight disadvantage where cricket was concerned but a big benefit in the school swimming-pool where, as a team diver, I made a considerably smaller plop. 'Ducker', the school swimming-pool, was one of the largest and best equipped in Europe, a conspicuous exception to Harrow's generally primitive facilities. Strictly speaking, it was New Ducker; Old Ducker, the Old Duck Puddle, had been literally that, muddy, foul and full of water snakes. Neither ran to heated water, so in winter we took training trips down the Bakerloo Line to the Seymour Hall Baths where I first learnt to associate London with the idea of dangerous, illegitimate thrills, sneaking off to buy Woodbines from the little kiosk on the corner. (Heimann D., the captain of swimming, should have known better than to join me.)

Back at the school the authorities, for reasons best known to themselves, had long since decided that Harrow lavatories would have no doors. And since none of us was allowed a bicycle, there were no bike sheds to nip round the back of. Our early experiments with the demon weed consequently took place in the open countryside that still surrounds the school, a fact which goes some way towards explaining why my great friend Player (who smoked Wills), my cousin Wills (who smoked Players) and I (who smoked whatever I could get) found ourselves one day half way up a tree as the bell for evening chapel sounded. Punctuality being the politeness of princes, we would normally not have dreamt of cutting things so fine; unfortunately, events had intervened in the form of a local courting couple who had arrived the moment we mounted our bosky eyrie and proceeded to court, rather vigorously we thought, at the base of it. We waited as long as we could but eventually could wait no longer, descending to materialise before their astonished eyes, raising our caps in polite apology as we stepped delicately over their recumbent forms.

Later still, on an illicit trip to the local newsreel cinema, another friend, Tedder, became so excited by Don Cockle's fight with Rocky Marciano that he stubbed his cigarette out on the fur coat of the lady in front, causing a noxious stink and a hurried exit. I have similar olfactory memories of another cinema visit, this time in the holidays, accompanying a friend of my sister whom I had marked down as the lucky recipient of my first mouth to mouth. I edged slowly closer and closer, adolescent blood pumping wildly, until finally I made my move, only to be promptly enveloped in a cloud of choking fumes from the commissionaire's pneumatic Flit Gun.

There were films at Harrow too, badly projected on to a tiny screen in the Speech Room; there were, however, quite definitely no girls. Harrow's original deed of endowment stipulated that 'they shall not receive any girl into the said school' (ironically, perhaps, given that the gift also included the parcel of land comprising Mayfair's notorious Shepherd Market) and more than two hundred years later the stipulation remained inviolate. The only girls we saw were the maids, and we made sure we saw as much of them as possible, crawling across endless expanses of flat roof to watch them change for bed. I have seen, in the course of my professional career, not a few young women without their clothes; not one of them has matched the maids of Harrow for erotic *élan*.

And so, slowly, we ached towards maturity, sneaking away to London at every possible opportunity, looning around the streets of Soho waiting for Experience to tap us on the shoulder and settling for a skiffle group in a milk bar instead.

The ultimate rite of passage was the annual Eton versus Harrow cricket match, a two-day school holiday which the senior boys traditionally spent with their parents in London. At the match itself, we spent most of our time standing under spiral staircases looking up women's skirts; it was the evenings that were earmarked for sophistication. Byron got drunk after he attended the match, and so did I, proudly wearing my first dinner jacket and accompanying my father to supper at the Savoy where the cabaret band was led by Roberto Inglis. The smell of cigarette smoke on that dinner jacket next morning was like a message from the gods: adulthood, finally, was just around the corner.

My father took the opportunity of introducing me to his fiancée, Monica Holdsworth-Hunt, a high-spirited woman who had had several husbands including, it transpired, the aforesaid Roberto Inglis; I pondered how I felt about being related by marriage to a band-leader and decided that, all in all, I rather liked the idea, even though my own tastes ran more to jazz bands than dance bands.

Although I saw my parents in equal proportion after the divorce, the time I spent with my mother remains most vividly in my memory, unsurprisingly, perhaps, given that she was now living in Paris. She, too, had remarried, choosing not a band-leader but a prince: Prince Georg of Denmark, a middle-aged and rather strait-laced career diplomat with an endless appetite for military music. As the wife of the Danish Military Attaché to the French, my mother now found herself with the perfect opportunity to exercise her expertise as the perfect hostess, a role which demanded skill, courage and *savoir faire*, particularly on the evenings when De Gaulle himself came to dinner. The chef (who, being both brilliant and French, was understandably prone to aberration) once prepared Langoustines Copenhagen; prepared but, for some extraordinary reason of his own, not actually cooked, so that the conversation around the table grew increasingly fevered as the guests fought to ignore the spastic waving of twenty little pink tails.

My French benefited considerably from these Parisian holidays, especially as my mother insisted on sending Liz and me out to do the shopping on our own. But when the lists got mixed

Shugborough as it is today

My great-grandfather photographed by Julia Margaret Cameron in 1871

My great-great-grandparents (second and fourth from the left) and my great-grandfather in velvet costume and hat (foreground) at Shugborough

With my father on the lawn at Shugborough

I am on the right of the photograph as a page
at my Aunt Betty's wedding, 1944

I am the aspiring soldier,
standing behind my grandfather

Liz and I, 1946

My sister and I walking near
Shugborough, with the head keeper
and Nanny Maxim

Aged nine

My leaving photograph at
Harrow

Back row extreme right in
1957, before the Regular
Commissions Board

With my father and grandfather at Shugborough

In the Camerouns with Sergeant Bailey

A ball at Blenheim. From left to right: Serena Russell,
the author, Lord Charles Spencer-Churchill and Alicia Barclay

Ascot. From left to right: The author, Prince Rainier of Monaco,
Princess Grace and Princess Marina, Duchess of Kent

A jazz club in the early Sixties

Left to right: David Bailey, Penelope Tree and the author

The author is second from the left in the front row; on the extreme right of the front row the Earl of Denbigh (photographed by Dmitri Kasterine)

My first team with Elizabeth Ramsay and Johnny Encombe

Left to right: the author, Count Arnaud de Ronay and Baron Alexis Waldeck, 1980, all hired by the legendary Diana Vreeland

Allegra Carracciolo and the author in the Bahamas, 1968

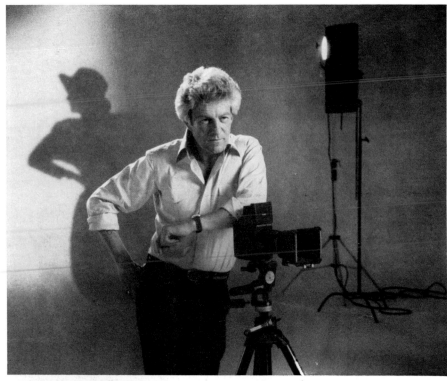

Making a commercial, Sydney, 1986

Recreating Victoriana

1974: my first Burberry suit

Dressed up for an Olympus
commercial

A photographic assignment with boutique partner Janet Lyle
and designer Michael Fish

up one day my linguistic confidence shrivelled and died as I found myself, like a man in an H. M. Bateman cartoon, silencing an entire *pharmacie* with a loud but faultlessly pronounced request for what I now know to be an extremely intimate item.

If, by some unlikely stroke of fate, my grandfather had found himself in Paris with me I like to think he might have completed my education in the recognised Edwardian manner by buying me a *poule de luxe*; luckily for everybody, though, he remained firmly ensconced at Shugborough, which was now under a new mistress, my step-grandmother, Violet, a strong character with a martial bearing and a refined profile. I scandalised my father by remarking that she reminded me of Field Marshal Montgomery in a skirt; we did not always get on.

I escaped as often as I could, which meant almost constantly, into the surrounding countryside, learning my way around the apparently boundless estate under close scrutiny from various gamekeepers and the more distant aegis of my grandfather.

One day he called me to one side after breakfast: 'New man, not sure of him. Put him through his paces, hm?' The new keeper, whose name I soon discovered to be Tracey, proved to be immediately likable and we spent the day in animated conversation trudging the length and breadth of the estate searching desperately for something we could take back to my grandfather. We returned as night fell: 'Right. Let's see how you got on.' My new friend, as anxious as I was to make a good impression, tipped out the game bag on to the boot-room floor with a dramatic flourish. And out crawled a small bewildered-looking pheasant that twitched, blinked and then staggered rapidly out of the door, taking my reputation with it.

Another new man arrived just in time to be pressed into service as wicket-keeper in the village cricket match; the first ball landed straight on his toe causing an over-explicit expletive that sent my grand-father straight back to the house in horror.

[ 33 ]

It was my father's soldier-servant, Percy Hancy, whom twenty years later I rediscovered working as a postman. His services as chauffeur-valet have proved indispensable ever since, as have his highly idiosyncratic wit and loyal cheerfulness.

On the rare days when the weather was bad enough to keep me indoors, I would wander round the huge and increasingly empty house, now unmistakably entering a period of steep decline. When things got particularly boring I would play ping-pong with myself, testing the various vertical surfaces for acoustic quality and degree of bounce. I settled eventually on one of a pair of eighteenth-century landscapes by Francesco Zuccarelli, R.A., whose canvas seemed to offer the perfect target.

It took me hours to perfect just the right amount of top spin required to return the ball neatly to my feet and I was interrupted only when my grandmother came charging in to drag me off by the scruff of the neck, demanding to know what I thought I was doing. Did I know how old that painting was? Had I no respect for quality and craftsmanship? Did my heritage mean nothing to me? I hung my head and mumbled in sincere shame as I was sentenced to a week without shooting, a week that I spent worrying about my lack of feeling for the finer things in life.

Years afterwards the painting was discovered to be a fake.

# [ 3 ]

My grandfather, despite having been Acting Master of Horse to the Lord Lieutenant of Ireland, was not a particularly military man; during the First World War he was a captain in the 5th City of London Rifles. My father, a Lieutenant Colonel in the Grenadiers, owed his length of Army service more, I think, to my grandfather's longevity than to any implicit love of soldiering.

Nonetheless it was with no sense of surprise that I found myself signing the application form for the Royal Military Academy, Sandhurst; it had long since been agreed that, after Harrow, a spell in the Army would do the boy no harm at all and might actually do him some good. The only other even marginally possible alternative was to spend two years studying Estate Management at the Agricultural College in Cirencester, a course of action I found totally unexciting; if the Harrow Cadet Corps was anything to go by I might at least find Sandhurst amusing.

The worst thing about the Corps was the uniform, an itchy, ill-fitting and deeply unsavoury assortment of crumpled khaki that was dragged reluctantly, each Thursday afternoon, out from amongst the uneaten food parcels and sweaty games clothes beneath my bed. The best thing was the opportunity to escape, for one week in the year, from both school and family to play soldiers at an Army camp near Folkestone where the alphabetically-allocated accommodation consisted of an endless row of six-man tents. I shared with Anderson, Ainsley, Angus, Alexander and Abdullah.

The last was a very haughty son of a sheik whom we decided,

adolescent prigs that we were, to be in urgent need of taking down a peg or two; shortly before bicycle drill, we fixed his brakes. The order came, ' 'Pare to mount . . . Mount!' and off we wobbled down the hill with Abdullah, who had never ridden anything other than a camel or a Cadillac before, taking an early lead. He lasted approximately seven seconds before disappearing into a large hole in the road, severely alarming six sleeping navvies.

Our punishment was to wash up: two thousand five hundred plates, spoons, knives and forks. After the first two or three hundred plates, when I noticed that the grease on the surface of the washing-up vats was by now probably thick enough to skate on and certainly thick enough to hide a good few thousand plates, spoons etcetera from the casual glance of the orderly in charge, I proposed an alternative plan of action to my companion, Brian Alexander, son of one of England's greatest Field Marshals.

Our punishment for that was orderly duty in the officers' latrines, a crude but relatively effective arrangement of pierced wooden seats ranged over a stream and shielded from the public view by a length of canvas. The busiest time seemed to be post-breakfast when, newspapers in hand, the officers arrived to spend the odd quarter of an hour mulling over world affairs in general, and England's progress in the Test Match in particular. Nobody paid us the slightest bit of attention as we soaked a large quantity of newspaper in paraffin, set it gently on the water upstream, lit the corner and retired to a safe vantage point. A row of flat hats was just visible above the top of the canvas screen. As the burning raft floated away from the bank, the first flat hat could be seen tilting gently to sniff the air before dipping back momentarily to the Test score, then rising very rapidly indeed to reveal the extremely startled face beneath it. As the first flat hat disappeared beneath the canvas, moaning gently, the third could be seen sniffing as the second rose, shrieking, into the air. And so it went on, sniff, shriek, moan, all the way down the line, officer after officer bobbing up and down like a multiple military jack-in-the-box, the whole sequence given added piquancy by the stoic immobility of the last hat in the row, entirely innocent of the nemesis progressing majestically downstream towards him. It was a deeply cinematic experience.

The other major event in the Cadet Corps calendar was the day when Brian's father came down to review the fledgling troops. The Field Marshal turned steadily from pink to mauve to puce as the entire affair rapidly degenerated into a complete shambles, with cadets bumping into each other, rifles dropping like hailstones and the sergeant-major bursting into tears. After a short speech in which the Field Marshal complimented us on providing him with a new low-point in his career, one of his immaculately-dressed A.D.C.s took me gently to one side and proceeded to wipe the grin off my face; he'd heard I was going to Sandhurst and then on to the Grenadiers; he thought I should know that this was not a decision to be taken lightly. Once I'd signed the application form I'd be committed – two years at Sandhurst, five years in the Brigade of Guards; difficult to get into either, impossible to get out. There were no conscripts at Sandhurst, and no National Servicemen, only serious volunteers, ambitious, dedicated, and intolerant of time-wasters. In short, one didn't just drift into Sandhurst, one jumped. And the harder one jumped, the further one got.

There are two mandatory requirements for cadets wishing to enter Sandhurst: high pass marks in the Civil Service Exam and a satisfactory report from the Regular Commissions Board. It was the former, a sort of A-level with knobs on, that gave me the most headaches, sitting it with a group of my friends at Kensington Town Hall, only to be informed afterwards that, as I should have been at Burlington House, I had in effect failed.

[ 37 ]

I added orienteering to my revision curriculum and tried again, passing gratefully six months later.

The remaining hurdle, the Regular Commissions Board, was much more my kind of thing: a whole day spent on and around an assault course at Westbury, our every move analysed and assessed for what it indicated about our moral character. I took no chances, nonetheless, spending several hours a day practising my impromptu five-minute speech ('Trout-Fishing Flies and How To Tie Them') and studying endless newspaper articles about Suez in order to ensure that I had something on which to Express an Opinion. The other part of the R.C.B., which consisted mainly of challenges that began 'You have three short planks, four jerry cans, a piece of rope, a thermometer and five minutes in which to ferry your platoon safely across this imaginery crocodile-infested river', seemed impossible to actually prepare for, so I simply worried a lot about it instead.

In the event, I lost only two men to the crocs and, despite giving an otherwise immaculate lecture on Tie-Flying, my character, hand-built at Harrow, was deemed to have passed the grade. I allowed myself a small glow of pride; for perhaps the first time in my life I'd achieved something for myself by myself. I wasn't drifting into Sandhurst and, more to the point, I wasn't being pushed; I was jumping.

I took a long time to land. At Sandhurst the Army needed just eighteen minutes to transform the smug, adolescent Hon. Patrick Anson that entered one end of the induction centre into the stooped, haggard 23528900 Cadet Anson that staggered out of the other, equipped with a rifle, a kit bag and barely any hair; and then things started to really move. B.R.C., Breakfast Roll Call, was at 6.15 each morning followed by breakfast, an hour's drill, an hour's teaching, an hour's P.T., lunch, games, more drill, tea, more lessons, supper, lights out, bed. Even moments of relaxation whilst we waited for our next instructor were heavily regulated: 'First man under that tree and smoke, move!'

The only pause in this endless activity was the brief hour before lights out, never quite long enough to contain all of the cleaning, washing, sewing, polishing and pressing required before the next morning's inspection. These sessions, spent sitting astride my narrow bed, were where I got to know my room-mate, a policeman's son from Brixham called Bloxham who had been most alarmed when I unpacked the new dinner jacket to which I'd treated myself, thinking it an item of uniform he'd neglected to procure. That dinner jacket got very little use that first year but, hanging in the plywood wardrobe, it remained a useful symbol, a sign that there were other things in life besides sweat, serge and sergeants.

Boots were the worst; there were twice as many opinions on the correct cleaning procedure as there were cadets but the consensus view seemed to be that one should begin with a hot teaspoon, smoothing out all the minute corrugations on the toe-cap into a thick flat sheet of leather which was then liberally smeared with several coats of spit and polish (the former ideally containing Mars Bar for added body) before being endlessly, endlessly rubbed to an eye-dazzling shine. When the tops of the boots seemed satisfactory, one moved on to the bottoms, bringing them back to reflective brilliance before finally, meticulously, polishing the thirteen metal studs on each sole.

When we cheated one inspecting officer by passing the same two pairs of boots through windows and behind backs from cadet to cadet all the way down the corridor, it became apparent that perfection was a flexible concept. There were high standards for everybody, but even higher ones for those who hoped to join a Guards regiment, particularly if that regiment was the same as the one in which the officer himself had enrolled.

The real power at Sandhurst rested with the sergeants-major, not the commissioned officers; fearsome, eagle-eyed martinets who knew a hundred ways to humiliate: the ear-shrivelling shout ('The third man from the right in the second platoon of Waterloo Company has got MIN CREAM ON HIS BOOTS!!!'), the casually spoken command (to King Hussein of Jordan: 'Stand still you idle little monarch.') and the deeply withering whisper ('I know we're going into the Grenadiers, sir, but we don't want to start growing our bearskin just yet, do we?'). We called them sir and they called us sir, and we were the ones who meant it.

The sergeant-major of sergeants-major was J. C. Lord ('He's the Lord up there and I'm the Lord down here stand up STRAIGHT!!'), a tall, elegant, much bemedalled man whose reputation was enough to start a nervous tremor in the ranks even before he rounded the corner onto the parade ground. Under his tyrannical direction we marched, counter-marched, wheeled, turned, saluted, stood to attention, stood at ease and stood easy (but never for long), developing calluses on our calluses as we turned, inexorably, from gawky adolescents into perfectly formed components in a well-oiled military machine.

Although I was careful to keep my hand in as far as the boxing went, the training I had in the ring was utterly outweighed by the unrelenting physical testing we were subjected to, each day, every day, hiking for miles in full kit across country or running round the parade ground for an hour at a time, pausing every ten minutes to do forty press-ups. I became, unsurprisingly, very fit very fast, relishing the challenge, liking it more the harder it got.

And it did get harder, particularly off the parade ground. In addition to all the obvious subjects like map-reading, radio procedure and military history, Sandhurst set a hard pace for academic work, particularly in Modern Languages, Science and Law; I found myself stretched, not only physically, but academically as well.

[ 40 ]

We worked hard and we played hard; games took on a fiercely competitive edge, particularly the regular intake races where one entire company would race another across a five-mile assault course. Here as elsewhere, Teamwork was the key concept with the moral laureate going to the first man lucky (or clever) enough to break through the finishing tape with an exhausted Malaysian team-mate carried protectively under his arm. Our shared experience of the system and our shared determination to outwit it created in us a genuine, and almost impenetrable, sense of *camaraderie*. We were, after all, volunteers not conscripts; a military élite, the best, not just in Britain, but in the whole wide world. Those of us destined for Guards regiments were more arrogant still: we were an élite within an élite. As our second year dawned and we were increasingly allowed out to exercise our egos on the unsuspecting streets, we formed a tightly-knit and increasingly dangerous little band of brothers.

Restricted initially to the neighbouring town of Camberley, we began by occupying the local greasy spoon, working our way steadily through all possible permutations of egg, chips, sausage, bacon, peas, mushrooms, baked beans, fried bread and fried tomatoes. Although pubs were distinctly out of bounds, every now and again we'd decide that rules were made to be broken and go off to get falling-down drunk. Inside Sandhurst, the strongest thing we drank was our nightly allowance of half a pint of pale ale, usually stretched with copious amounts of lemonade to provide at least a pint of shandy; outside Sandhurst, we discovered that the consequence of abstention was the ability to achieve almost total alcoholic collapse very cheaply, rarely requiring more than one large vodka.

I discovered that Bloxham, in particular, became a desperate man when drunk, ready, willing and completely unable to take on any man in the bar; my effective but inelegant solution was to render him prematurely unconscious with a tap on the jaw, a tactic which I regret to say cost him several teeth. Towards the end of one particularly excessive debauch (two vodkas) we decided to enliven the coming Bank Holiday weekend by altering the road signs on the nearby A30, diverting several resorts-worth of traffic into Sandhurst itself, promoting picknicking on the firing range, paddling in the assault course and the setting up of deckchairs all over the hallowed parade ground.

The danger to the public escalated exponentially as we began to acquire cars, sold to us at what we were told were knock-down prices by the newly-qualified cadets in the year above us. Bernadine (after a Pat Boone song) cost me £15 and she was the most beautiful car in the world – a 1938 M.G. PA. I'd already scared a lot of sheep at Shugborough learning to manoeuvre the heavy Buick up and down the drive; Bernadine, no longer entirely in the first flush of youth, was much more interesting to drive being both less heavy and less well maintained. I tried to imagine Rose gauging the amount of fuel remaining to him using only a tightly rolled brolly stuck into the petrol tank, and failed. Sandhurst had, of course, taught us the rudiments of motor mechanics (indeed rather more, given that we once managed to completely strip down one flash captain's flash Austin Healey Sprite before reconstructing it again in his bedroom); the basic theory was now supplemented with an intensive course in practical maintenance, particularly where retreading retread tyres with a penknife was concerned.

None of this, or petty technicalities like driving licences or road tax, deterred me from whistling down to visit my sister at her school, or from striking sporty poses in front of her impressionable young friends. But London was where the real action was, of that we remained certain. And, by and large, we got there, often in one piece, despite having done the entire journey in twenty-nine minutes forty-five and a half seconds. As at Harrow, the sinful city that we knew was out there somewhere singularly failed to materialise and we spent much of our precious free time playing silly games in Hyde Park and Belgrave Square, charging round and round at hair-raising speeds, endangering life, limb and ratable values. I could even, eventually, boast of having been stopped for speeding whilst postponing an overdue visit to my grandmother endlessly circling the wedding-cake-like sculpture group outside Buckingham Palace (I usually omitted to mention the speed involved, 35 m.p.h. being generally considered a risible minimum rather than an endorsable maximum).

Equally thrilling, but considerably less devastating to the general public, was parachute jumping. We called ourselves the Teddy Bear Club, after the small mascot we used to throw out before us, usually, but not always, equipped with his own little parachute. Naturally enough we were intrigued by the opportunities for derring-do presented by the *Daily Mail*'s announcement of a London/Paris Air Race. So, it seemed, was half the population of Europe but as our motorbikes roared us away from the starting-point at the Arc de Triomphe we were delighted to find ourselves quickly alone on the road, then less delighted to find ourselves in fact on the wrong road.

Finding a pilot to fly us to England from the tiny airfield we'd selected took us not all that much longer than we'd expected and even the subsequent attentions of the Excisemen of Hornchurch didn't seem to slow us down substantially. Our ongoing progress was smoothed by numerous three-man support teams waiting at strategic traffic lights: two scouts (one looking out for us, the other looking out for the police) and a heavy, whose sole role was to simulate heavy traffic by jumping up and down on the hydraulic control strips to ensure a constant green. As we sped towards Marble Arch, steeling ourselves to resist the blandishments of fame yet again, we were puzzled to discover no cheering crowds, no bunting and no finishing line. A road

[ 43 ]

sweeper, pausing amidst a mountain of discarded programmes, informed us that everybody had long since gone home having applauded the award of prizes to the R.A.F., a millionaire in a private helicopter and a nun on a motor-mower.

As our last year moved steadily towards its close, it became increasingly apparent that only a major disaster could interfere with our glorious onward and upward progress and we began to stay out all night, returning bleary-eyed for Breakfast Roll Call. My grandfather's wind-up gramophone had proved invaluable when Liz and I decided to teach ourselves to dance in the holidays; now she was a debutante, one of the last to be actually presented at Court, and beginning to go to coming-out balls. Naturally she needed a chaperone; naturally it was me.

Those deb dances were, for a while at least, sheer magic; acre upon acre of pink chiffon and starched cotton effortlessly ebbing and flowing, throwing up here a familiar face, there an interestingly unfamiliar face, the whole in constant motion all the while until I began to feel myself in serious danger of becoming socially seasick. I discovered that the extra cost of laundering and relaundering stiff white shirts and waistcoats could be more than matched by the potential savings on food bills, particularly if one could stick it out until the traditionally lavish breakfasts were served at dawn. I danced with literally hundreds of girls, kissed quite a few of them and even, in some cases, managed a little polite conversation. I told nobody that my father had recently gone into hospital, having been stung by a bee.

The Passing Out parade that marked my formal leave-taking of Sandhurst was a proud moment for me, made even more entertaining by the friskiness of the adjutant's horse. The adjutants at Sandhurst are always footguards rather than cavalrymen and the mere sight of a horse tends to make them uneasy, particularly in front of royalty and hundreds of proud parents. This particular horse, although it had spent the previous twenty-four hours under armed guard to prevent laxatives being smuggled into its nosebag, seemed distinctly footloose.

Despite the solemnity of the occasion, I had several times noticed a suppressed giggle sweeping the ranks as the adjutant fought nervously for control. Finally, the horse could stand it no longer and, at the climactic moment when the passing-out cadets are supposed to sweep up the steps and out of sight for ever, it bolted. Rapidly developing an alarming turn of speed it galloped furiously several times around the parade ground with the adjutant hanging on for dear life. And then, as suddenly as it had started, it stopped. The adjutant, mind visibly working overtime, looked down at the entirely innocent cadet in front of whom he'd chanced to halt. 'Sergeant-Major, take this man's name,' he said and without further ado trotted demurely back to resume his position at the head of the parade.

I found myself wishing that my father could have been there to appreciate this display of *sang froid*; given that I was now an Under-Officer, he might even have considered restraining himself from lecturing me on my levity and laughed with me instead. But the humorous bee sting had, by some one-in-a-million chance, caused an entirely inappropriate allergic reaction; he had died, aged forty-four, on 14th March 1958 in King Edward VII's Hospital.

His obituary notices underlined a side of his character that I myself had often seen, and envied: 'From the sandy wastes of the Northern Desert to the comfort of his club, Bill Anson's ability to use laughter to lighten potential dangers brought him many friends from every walk of life.'

I would have liked him to have lightened my life now and again; I would have liked to be able to remember him as a friend as much as a father. But that was asking the impossible; he was always too deeply ambitious on my behalf to risk confusing me with affection. After he died, many of his friends told me how

[ 45 ]

proud he'd been of my small achievements. I wonder what he would make of me now.

Liz took his death particularly badly; helping her to cope with her grief helped me to cope with mine. At Shugborough, the loss of an heir hastened the house's almost Dickensian decline. My grandparents, continuing the process of retrenchment that had begun with the war, had slowly evacuated one gloomy room after another until now they were virtually camping out in the sole remaining heated room with only a housekeeper for company.

Something would have to be done about that, presumably by me. But not yet; I had a regiment to join.

# [ 4 ]

Most of my father's Army uniform, including the bearskin, fitted
me pretty well but a few items still needed to be specially made;
I spent much of my last few weeks of Sandhurst at Messrs Johns
and Pegg in Clifford Street, being fitted for my service dress
with its lone star sewn proudly on the shoulders. My attitude to
joining the Grenadiers had by now settled down into a mixture
of mild excitement and total terror, emotions that were only
slightly calmed by the still small voice inside me that kept
insisting it was only a job like any other. Socially there would,
no doubt, be the usual rituals to be learnt, the usual arcane
terminology to be mastered, and as a new boy once again I could
also look forward to a certain amount of ragging but I knew how
to handle that by now.

I had already enjoyed a preliminary visit to the Officers' Mess
at Chelsea Barracks for the traditional pre-induction dinner, an
elaborate and highly elegant *soirée* that had ended at midnight
with brandy snaps and coffee. Eagle-eyed hospitality on the one
hand and nervous tension on the other had combined to ensure
that I was, by that stage, more than a little drunk. It was with
only minimal embarrassment that I heard myself telling, for the
umpteenth time that year, my King George VI funeral story, the
one where Liz and I waved so frantically at my father (one of
the marshals in charge of the parade) that he was forced to wave
his baton in reply, thereby inadvertently signalling his troops to
quick march the next two hundred yards.

As I wittily described the subsequent military concertina that for me had been the high point of the whole affair, I stabbed my fork emphatically into a brandy snap, which promptly cracked open with a loud report and skittered wildly across the highly polished dining table to land in the Commanding Officer's lap.

A wise young officer having taken the basic precaution of removing the distributor cap from my car, I had ample time to reflect on my various gaffes as I staggered home in the rain. I was familiar enough with the Army's little ways to realise that I had been expected to make a fool of myself; anything less and I would have labelled myself a prig. The malice that I thought I'd occasionally detected amongst my fellow guests was surely attributable to paranoia on my part; besides, the next time I met these people they would be not fellow-guests but fellow-officers, fellow-officers and fellow-gentlemen.

The first indication of the depth of my foolishness came when I found myself ordered to report, not to Chelsea, but to Tidworth. As I knew, but had obviously failed to comprehend, the Grenadiers had two separate battalions which alternated between ceremonial duties in London and tactical work elsewhere. I was wanted in Wiltshire and to Wiltshire I went, driving smartly through the barrack gates and straight into the parade ground, stopping only to enquire of a passing officer the whereabouts of the Mess. Blinded by apprehension, I completely failed to notice that he was in charge of a parade at the time, a parade which was having considerable difficulty negotiating a path around my parked car. That was the first time I was shouted at in the Grenadiers; it was far from the last.

As I settled myself in, I was more than a little alarmed to see that Tidworth took itself very seriously, going about its business with a gravity that was only partially explained by the low-level alert that coincided with my arrival. My first few months were spent in intensive preparation for anti-guerrilla warfare: minimum support, maximum discomfort, planning and executing a complex series of night exercises and twenty-five-mile route-marches carrying everything we needed on our backs.

I also discovered just how average the average Guardsman could be. Sandhurst had equipped us perfectly for a career which might eventually lead to the command of a company, a battalion or even, in time, the entire brigade. But it had given us no experience whatsoever of dealing with the Common Soldier, compared with whom even the most slovenly officer cadet seemed like a paragon of ambition, initiative and intelligence. Their sadly unsparkling boots alone bore ample testimony to the fact that the average Guardsman was a conscript, not a volunteer.

I found myself, utterly unprepared, in sudden charge of twenty men, most of whom had begun shaving whilst I was still dallying with Miss G.; fully grown adults who'd married at eighteen and divorced at twenty; case-hardened veterans who knew every trick in the book and not a few beyond it. They were absolutely terrifying.

Luckily for everyone concerned, each platoon was equipped with its own interpreter, the Platoon Sergeant. I had the particular good fortune to work with Sergeant Bailey (no relation), a man who, by dint of much discreet whispering in my ear and an impressive repertoire of subtle grimaces, managed to avert us from near disaster more than once. (He was otherwise remarkably untypical: he addressed me, invariably, as 'Kind Young Sir' and was himself known to the rest of the platoon as 'Uncle Charles'.)

The men were bad news but the officers were even worse. Public interaction with senior personnel was usually confined, on my part, to a snappy salute acknowledging orders received and understood. Privately, in the Mess, things were a little more complicated. Army officers in general, and Grenadiers in particular, have a long and glorious history of defending the *status quo* against attack from outside; they have an inbred distrust of change. Tradition, yet again, was all.

I learnt their little ways as I had learnt Harrow's little ways: slowly, painfully, and not without a great deal of embarrassment. The dinner table, in particular, was a social minefield, liberally seeded with unspoken custom and taboo. Caps were always worn at table (which would have shocked Nanny). Christian names were used at all times, except when addressing the Commanding Officer, who was always Sir. And nobody, but nobody, left the table before he did, or until the port had circulated at least three times.

Worst by far was the unwritten rule that new officers must remain strictly incommunicado for their first six weeks in the Mess. Blithely unaware of this, I breezed into my first breakfast determined to present a cheerful, chipper and distinctly chatty persona. My loud good mornings having met with a solid wall of silence, I changed tack and moved on to the weather.

'Lovely morning!' I said to a captain helping himself to scrambled egg. 'Glorious day,' I warbled at a major over the orange juice. No response. I determined on one last try as I eased myself into my seat at the breakfast table.

'Hope the rain holds off . . . ?' The silence was broken only by the rustle of newsprint as my neighbour lowered his newspaper to fix me with a basilisk stare. He rose slowly to his feet, picked up his fork and banged it, gavel-like, on the mahogany.

'Gentlemen. Lord Anson wishes to address the Mess on the subject of the weather,' he announced, and sat down again. It was the last time I ever attempted to force a conversation.

This silent period was of course designed to allow the officer corps to meditate undisturbed on the thorny question of whether the new boy was, or was not, One of Us, an extremely important consideration in such a tightly knit society where there was everywhere an acute apprehension that there were two ways of doing things, Ours and the rest. 'They' might refer casually to a C.O. or an R.S.M.; we knew them by their proper names: the Commanding Officer and the Regimental Sergeant-Major. Officers in other regiments had batmen to look after them but we had soldier servants. (And I had Guardsman Carver who, when an early-morning mug of tea failed to rouse me, would stick a freshly lit Capstan Extra Strength in my mouth, bringing me coughing into instant consciousness.) We did not have First or Second Lieutenants as the others did; we had Ensigns and Subalterns.

As the most junior of all the Ensigns I spent a lot of time on Picket Duty, an extremely boring round of undemanding petty tasks considered so mind-numbingly tedious that it was otherwise reserved as a punishment for infractions of the code. Unaware of the low regard in which my post was held and charged with a heady sense of responsibility, I spent my first day as Picket Officer frantically consulting my duty roster, working my way steadily through the day's events from '0600 hours: See Up Men's Breakfast' to '2300 hours: Close Sergeants Mess'. The latter should have been comparatively easy, requiring no more than the huge self-confidence needed to announce 'Gentlemen, I wish to close the bar' to a large room full of inebriated senior N.C.Os.

But they too had an initiation ceremony for young officers, requiring them to stand on the bar and down a pint mug containing one measure of every single spirit in the place garnished, as often as not, with the contents of one large ashtray. The trick, I dimly recognised as I staggered back to my room, was not to throw up until one was well out of sight. The parade ground remained unblemished by a matter of a split second or two; my drum kit had to be hosed down with disinfectant.

Jazz drumming, a habit I'd got into during my last few months at Sandhurst, was a wonderful way of venting my mounting frustrations and the two or three hours I now spent every night accompanying Chris Barber, Ottilie Patterson, and Miles Davis split my fellow junior officers into two distinct camps: those who spent their time shouting rude comments and banging on the walls and the others, far fewer, who came to see what was going on and stayed to listen (to my records rather than my drumming I need hardly add).

One of them was Algy Cluff (who subsequently gained some fame first as an oil man and then the proprietor of the *Spectator*). Algy, despite having emerged from a relatively ordinary background, looked every inch the Grenadier, tall, thin and very elegant; he was also, as we were to discover later, an extremely good soldier. Even more to my liking, he was an extremely serious eccentric; I remember him returning to the Mess in high dudgeon one day after some imagined slight, walking very deliberately down a long line of regulation bowler hats, lifting each one from its peg, turning it over and ramming it, forcefully, inside out.

Another friend I made at this time was a great practical joker who was romancing a girl who lived in the country with her widowed mother, a lady with a passion for petit-point. When he discovered Brown & Pontings disappearing ink the temptation was too great. 'Mother at her tapestry, self writing letters, self's young lady serving tea when suddenly, oops, ink all over needlework. Disaster! Frantic looks criss-cross mother's crest-fallen head. Old lady groans, young lady mutters imprecations, self mumbles apologies, deep shame etcetera until, just as suddenly, ink disappears! Relief! Joy! Mystery! Self confesses, little prank, ho ho, all parties laugh heartily, mother returns to needlework whilst self and self's young lady repair elsewhere for happy and hopefully passionate reconciliation! Can't fail.'

He returned that evening a mere shadow of his former self.

Having spilt the ink, he'd spent the first ten minutes apologising profusely as planned and had then decided, as the trick seemed to be working a little slowly, to explain all. For the next half hour he, his girlfriend and his girlfriend's mother had sat in silence as the ink slowly dried into an ineradicable stain; we'd exchanged his Brown & Pontings for a bottle of Quink Permanent Blue.

The third, and closest, friend I made was a rogue called Nicholas Villiers who was already famous for having once kept a girl in the Mess for several weeks, feeding her on smuggled cake and taking her out on exercises. He and I shared a passionate interest in two things, Jazz and Women, and we made a point of satisfying both interests regularly and, where possible, simultaneously. This policy set us even further apart from many of our colleagues in the Mess who seemed quite happy with their occasional visits to Mrs Featherstonehaugh's establishment for young ladies (and somewhat older gentlemen) somewhere in Knightsbridge.

One officer, returning from a spell of duty in Oman, was so understandably anxious to resume relations with the female of the species that he had but one thought on entering the Mess after more than two years away.

'Evening, chaps, I don't suppose anyone knows Ma Feathers' telephone number?'

There was a pause whilst all present pondered the advisability of admitting to such knowledge, a pause terminated only by the Commanding Officer speaking from behind his *Times*: 'Flaxman 2896.'

'Thanks, old bean,' replied the officer, clearly unaware of the identity of his informant. Later that night, the Commanding Officer's wife, fully briefed, encouraged the young man at the other end of the telephone line to give precise details of his requirements for over a quarter of an hour until her husband, bored with the joke, seized the phone, said something to the effect of 'Do shut up, Charles,' and replaced the receiver. Next morning, Charles bounced into breakfast, eager to impart his news.

'I say, chaps, you'll never guess what.'

'What?' we duly enquired.

'I rang Ma Feathers' last night. . . .'

'Yes?'

'And the Commanding Officer was in bed with her!'

Villiers and I lacked both the inclination and the money for Ma Feathers' and we were certainly not prepared to wait until our London tour of duty to start hitting the high spots.

Our nightly raids on the capital's clubland were soon cut short by a posting to Tripoli. The Army has a strictly ordered hierarchy of message codes, ranging from Unclassified through Restricted to Top Secret and beyond; the fastest and most serious of them all, reserved for generals and monarchs, is a 'Flash' which takes priority throughout the entire system and gets through in minutes. Villiers, who formed part of the advance party, left before I did and that night, since we were technically On Alert, I made sure I left details of my itinerary at the Guard Room before setting off for London on my own. Half way through the evening I was surprised to find myself called into the manager's office to take a telephone call.

'Lord Anson?' said the soldier at the other end of the line. 'Flash for you, sir.'

'Oh yes?' I said, giving a desperate imitation of a man who received Flash messages several times a night.

'What does it say?'

'Message reads: BRING MILES DAVIS ROUND ABOUT MIDNIGHT LOVE VILLIERS. Any reply, sir?'

I admired his taste. Had I found myself marooned in the desert and with the good fortune to discover not only a girl but also what was probably the only wind-up gramophone in North Africa, 'Round About Midnight' was probably the record I'd have most wanted. I denied any knowledge of either Villiers or Davis and returned to the dance floor, leaving an expert team of code-breakers at Southern Command to spend several months decoding what was obviously an invitation to a deeply suspicious late-night rendezvous.

At the end of the Tripoli exercise, Villiers and I, basking in new-found fitness after a series of fifteen-mile night marches across scorpion-infested deserts, decided we'd like to walk back to England, an ambitious plan of action that was foiled only by our Commanding Officer's 'No!' uttered decisively whilst we were still twenty yards away from explaining the idea. We walked instead to Cyrene, famous for its Roman ruins, where Villiers insisted on taking photographs of a long row of classical statues. We were deeply offended when, back in London, Wallace Heaton refused to process the film for fear of prosecution under the Obscene Publications Act. A long correspondence ensued in which we patiently explained that classical statues, being embodiments of everything that was Pure and Noble in Roman civilisation, were not supposed to have clothes on. The correspondence ended abruptly when it was pointed out that the third statue from the left was wearing an Army issue watch, and I never modelled for Villiers again.

Although I was still attending deb dances, they were beginning to pall a little by now, although things perked up when I plucked up the nerve to begin offering to replace the drummer in the dance band when he wanted a break. I discovered that all eligible young men were catalogued in a classified document known simply as 'The List'; when I finally got hold of a copy I was devastated to find that the only information against my name was the damning indictment 'N.S.I.T.': Not Safe in Taxis.

[ 55 ]

As the deb season ended, the shooting season began, and I found myself invited to various country house shoots, the social side of which, after a while, became just as boring as the dances. The same old faces turned up with the same old jokes and the same old deeply predictable diatribes, each of which always began 'The trouble with England. . . .' One particularly dull weekend reached its low point around three in the morning with the assembled guests braying hysterically on the perimeter of the pool, into which the usual hoorays were chucking the usual girls to the accompaniment of the usual hysterical shrieks and mindless laughter. Villiers and I strolled casually around the perimeter of the party, each of us unobtrusively carrying one end of a long length of hosepipe. At a given signal we tightened our noose, lassooing host, hostess and thirty or so guests into the pool.

I had a similarly visual revenge in the Mess one evening when a tableful of officers attempting to rise for the Loyal Toast found that their shoelaces had been knotted together under the table to form a continuous shackle. I was awarded several days' Picket Duty for that, a punishment that paled into insignificance before what was to come.

We had piled into my Austin Healey sharp on the dot of 1730 hours as usual, heading for London through some of the worst winter weather in several years. Villiers, who had displayed his usual infuriating habit of falling instantly asleep, had a rude awakening when we came over the top of a hill a split second too late to notice the huge lorry on the other side. It proceeded, very slowly as it seemed at the time, to cut the car into two neat halves. Alcohol being a known antidote for shock, I remember very little of the following evening except that it ended with Villiers and me being discovered in a Claridges Hotel room with two young women at five-thirty in the morning. Under normal circumstances we might still have made it back for Breakfast

Roll Call, but neither of us had remembered that we now had no car.

The barracks was deserted; the only incumbent the large and extremely irate Senior Major who reminded us that the whole battalion had that morning departed for manoeuvres before clapping us under House Arrest.

Villiers had an unnerving ability to come up pure as the driven snow in these circumstances, but even he got something terrible like ten days' Pickets. I got thirty but there was worse in store. When the rest of the battalion returned we were all sent off to join a major exercise on Salisbury Plain. Villiers and I had the singular honour of being chosen to be the enemy, two men against three regiments, trudging hither and thither through pouring rain for five days without sleep carrying radio sets, planting signals and generally messing things up (a role which, it must be said, suited us rather well). As we lay exhausted one morning watching the sun edging above the horizon, I indulged myself in the vision of the perfect breakfast; fresh orange juice of course, poached eggs on a lightly toasted muffin, some crisply fried bacon perhaps and definitely a lot of very hot, very strong coffee.

I turned to Villiers, prone in the bracken beside me: 'What would you most like to see when you next open your eyes?'

He groaned and raised himself briefly on one elbow whilst he thought about it.

'Sophia Loren's bum,' he said and collapsed again.

As our London tour grew closer and closer, one thing was becoming increasingly clear: we had to have a flat.

My girlfriend at the time, an extremely attractive girl called Jennifer Wontner, had a father, Sir Hugh, who was chairman of the Savoy. One evening, after a splendid dinner during which I'd monopolised the conversation with a tedious diatribe on the awfulness of English cooking ('The trouble with England is . . .'), he took me to one side.

I expected to be interrogated about my intentions towards his daughter but, very much to my surprise, he offered me a job instead. In retrospect, I rather think I ought to have taken it but I was far more interested in something he'd said earlier about a block of semi-derelict property he'd just bought from the Grosvenor Estate (and on which he was later to build the Berkeley Hotel). Did it by any faint chance, seemed silly to ask really but you never know, won't ask doesn't get as Nanny used to say, were there any empty flats available? Indeed there were and, thanks to Sir Hugh's generosity, three friends and I moved into a crumbling but deceptively spacious two-bedroom flat in Wilton Place that very weekend, at a peppercorn rent of one pound nineteen shillings and sixpence a week.

We rapidly agreed to use one bedroom as a dormitory, thus leaving the other constantly available for maiden aunts who might find themselves in London for a little light shopping. To avoid disturbing the aunts unnecessarily, we also agreed a complex empty milk bottle code: one bottle for two hours, two bottles for four hours and so on. (Later, having left the flat expecting a thoroughly romantic evening with a girl of whom I had high hopes, I returned around midnight, depressed, frustrated and entirely alone, to find not one, not two, but three milk bottles outside the door. I spent six cold and lonely hours waiting for whoever it was to finish before finally, fatigue having triumphed over discretion, I let myself very quietly in to what turned out to be an utterly empty flat. The milk bottles had been mine.)

The flat rapidly established itself as an ideal base camp from which to plan our assault on London's nightlife. In those days even off-duty Guards officers were subject to a highly constricting code of conduct, prohibited from travelling anywhere by anything other than private car or taxi (no bikes and very definitely no buses) and forbidden to carry anything other than a tightly rolled black umbrella (which meant that an officer on guard at St James's Palace fancying a short swim at the R.A.C. Club pool had to be escorted the scant half mile up Pall Mall by his fully uniformed soldier servant, who walked one pace behind him carrying the bathing suit neatly bundled up in brown paper.) We were also expected to wear a bowler hat and a stiff white collar at all times; the flat proved the perfect place for me to garage my growing collection of distinctly non-regimental Levis.

More than that, however, it was my first real home. Better still, and even more seductive than the delights of the second bedroom, there was a spare bathroom: a tiny cupboard of a place over which I'd exercised an immediate *droit du seigneur*: my first darkroom.

Being able at last to process and print my own films proved a major revelation and I spent an increasingly pleasurable proportion of my spare time locked in the bathroom, turning out huge portrait prints of a succession of girlfriends which we used to decorate the sitting-room walls (which had to be laboriously scraped clean every time I altered my affections). My photography, which had languished at Sandhurst, now became much more than just a hobby; it was a passion. And, as with all passions, it learnt to thrive on denial; the Army, quite predictably, decided that I ought to begin to go on some courses.

I spent weeks staring at blackboards all over the country, always wanting to be in London and rarely managing to get there. My duties as Messing Officer took up what little spare time I did have in vain attempts to raise enough funds to send our Sergeant Cook for a couple of weeks' training at the Dorchester where I hoped to break him of his iron-clad allegiance to Beef Wellington and Baked Alaska. Liz, who'd followed in mother's footsteps by taking a series of extremely odd jobs (including a short but educative spell as afternoon receptionist at the Hyde Park Hotel), slipped a disc climbing awkwardly out of a taxi and, needing a sit-down job and having noticed the increasingly poor standards of catering at deb dances, she began a business of her own: the immensely successful Party Planners. She had considerably more success in the field than I did; for all I know Beef Wellington figures on regimental menus to this day.

As I became more at home in the Mess, the focus of my incipient paranoia shifted slightly. In any closed institution, the price paid for group solidarity is the creation of scapegoats, and for a while (a short while mercifully) it seemed to be me. My chief persecutor was a slippery figure called Drummond (not his real name), an objectionable hearty who had already given me a lot of trouble at Sandhurst, and who now seemed intent on ruining my performance on the parade ground; my boots developed inexplicable and ineradicable stains, my vehicle requisition chitties became mysteriously lost in transit and my men found themselves subjected to increasingly confusing but utterly untraceable series of orders and counter-orders. My retaliation was swift but unsubtle, owing much to the new training programme upon which I'd recently embarked. Hours spent skipping in the Boiler Room coupled with gargantuan meals of rump steak and Guinness meant I was now able to match Drummond on more or less equal terms and did so, often.

On our last night at Tidworth, a fierce fracas began with fists and ended with a fire bucket. As I sat in the Casualty Ward I realised that he had unwittingly done me a small favour; now I could visit Mr Birchet in the Waterloo Road.

The scar that would soon no doubt develop around thirty stitches in my forehead not only stood a good chance of being romantic rather than disfiguring ('Just a little duelling trophy . . .'); it also made nonsense of my father's oft-repeated lectures on distinguishing marks. The theory, which I'd never quite grasped, had something to do with not enabling the enemy to identify escapers; a macabre and, I always thought, faintly hypocritical attitude, given that both he and my grandfather bore rather striking tattoos – as did, even more oddly, several of my female relations including an aunt who had to spend much of her life in her lisle stockings when fashion decreed knee-length skirts that would have revealed the butterfly on her calf.

Now it was my turn; the scar faded in less than six months but Mr Birchet's tattoo, our family's seahorse emblem, is etched on my arm to this day.

# [ 5 ]

Nominally, at least, ceremonial duty implied an awesome responsibility: we were to defend, on Her Majesty's behalf, four of the most historic corners of the realm; the Bank of England, the Tower of London, St James's Palace and, of course, Buckingham Palace.

Each location proved equally pleasant, although reaching the Bank was something of an ordeal; it can be a long march from Wellington Barracks to the City, especially in the rain, and we were forbidden to stop for anyone or anything, thereby providing an all too tempting target for disaffected motorists. The newspaper vans in Fleet Street were a particular menace, although they would regret their *lèse-majesté* when we caught up with them at the traffic lights at the foot of Ludgate Hill; marching remorselessly past, my platoon (twenty minds with but a single thought – if that) would swing the butts of their shouldered rifles just a little more widely than usual, executing an immaculate, deafening and highly damaging drum roll along the entire length of the van.

The Tower, whence we travelled by truck, turned out to be almost village-like in atmosphere, especially after the tourists had gone home. For some curious reason, we were allowed to entertain girls in the Officers' Mess where the clock was always carefully kept at least a quarter of an hour slow; visitors who failed to make it to the gate by the stroke of midnight found themselves locked in tight for the night. The only nocturnal visitations I suffered were the occasional calls to the guard-room where I would stand, shivering in a greatcoat and trousers hastily slung over pyjamas, listening to yet another white-faced, chain-smoking guardsman describe his encounter with an invisible and unfriendly foe. ('It was a great big white thing which ignored my challenge so I threw my rifle at it, sah!')

Other than that, the most sinister things I saw at the Tower were the ravens, an ugly-looking mob of scavengers whose departure, legend has it, will signal the fall of the kingdom; the odds on this eventuality were lengthened by the authorities with a little judicious wing-clipping and shortened considerably by various other outrages on their persons, which included carrying the loyal birds, captured and anaesthetised by bread soaked in brandy, to the very top of the White Tower before unceremoniously chucking them over the parapet. ('Guardsman Average reporting. Ravens still able to fly, sah! Just.')

Ceremonially speaking, our *pièce de résistance* was the Ceremony of the Keys, a highly theatrical performance involving both Guardsmen and Beefeaters that inevitably drew large crowds.

The glamour of being the cynosure of every eye delighted me for approximately twenty-four hours before wearing off completely, never to return. I now had a new object on which to exercise my persecution complex: the public at large. We dreaded the arrival of the Americans in particular, each new coach-load marvelling loudly at our Wunnerful Heritage before quietly drawing us aside to make a substantial offer for our bearskins. They offered even more ridiculous prices for black market tickets to the Trooping of the Colour; we turned sternly away, unable to explain that we had already sold them to the doorman at the Dorchester. I agreed with Alice: a soldier's life is terrible hard.

The Americans, at least, took us seriously. The Great British Public, not without some justice, obviously thought of the silent sentries as a funfair sideshow. Make-The-Soldier-Move-and-Win-a-Goldfish brought out a surprisingly inventive streak in the G.B.P.; one young lady became a regular visitor, standing on tiptoe to whisper astonishingly graphic details of her love-life into a blushing guardsman's shell-like ear.

Unused to maintaining such a high profile, I began to think of myself as something of a bird in a gilded cage, a whimsical metaphor that gained extra point when we began performing behind the railings at Buckingham Palace; I kept expecting to be thrown a Bath bun.

The average guardsman, now relatively free from distractions, developed an alarming tendency to slip away into a standing coma, re-screening endless Cup Finals on the inside of his skull till all hours. One of my jobs was to make sure that someone was still at home somewhere inside his impressive uniform; a chore that was traditionally achieved by asking a series of time-honoured silly questions and receiving the time-honoured silly answers:

'Tell me, Guardsman Average, what would you do if you noticed the Palace was on fire?'

'Put it out, sah!'

'And how would you do that?'

'Piss on it, sah!'

Every now and again I'd attempt to liven things up by introducing a slightly more surreal note:

'Tell me, Guardsman Average, what would you do if you noticed a battleship coming up The Mall?'

'Shoot it dahn, sah!'

'And how would you do that?'

'Submarine, sah!'

'Yes, of course. And where would you get your submarine?'

'Same sodding stupid place you got your battleship from, sah!'

Over-confidence had already marred my first tour of duty at Buckingham Palace. Convinced that I knew all that I needed to know about the drill, I'd not bothered to rehearse and set off from Wellington Barracks in high spirits, leading off to the sound of the brass band playing my choice of March of the Day. (Rather than listen to yet another exquisite rendering of 'The British Grenadiers', I'd requested 'Clarinet Marmalade', an old Mick Mulligan number, and they were doing an excellent job on it.) As we drew alongside the Palace railings I noticed that the centre gates were already open. Although I vaguely recalled some tradition about always entering at the right-hand side, I persevered nonetheless, only to find that the gates had been opened not to celebrate First Lieutenant Viscount Anson's arrival, but to facilitate the departure of the Sovereign. I draw a swift and heavy veil over the chaos, shame and total degradation that ensued.

Once inside the gates, the procedure was much the same as at the Tower. The new guard carefully lined up opposite the old like two lines of chorus-boys. Centre stage the two soloists would bawl the ritual exchange into each other's faces:

'Who goes there?'

'The Keys!'

'Whose Keys?'

'The Queen's Keys!' and so on, culminating in the passing-over of said keys.

Happily for the kingdom, we were never entrusted with the Keys themselves, and were forced to make do with other tokens, usually something calculated to shatter the poker-like deportment of our opposite number: a teddy-bear, a banana, and even the occasional French letter all served their turn but the favourite by far was a very soft-boiled egg held together by only the thinnest membrane of carefully broken shell; many a uniform was ruined that way, and not a few reputations.

For my final Changing, however, I was delighted to find that I was scheduled to hand over to one Captain Drummond. After a lightning visit to the Household Goods Department of Bourne & Hollingsworth, twenty Capstan Full Strength persuaded Drummond's soldier servant to let me into his room. His heavy bearskin stood swathed in its customary protective armour of several damp tea towels and, with a glance at my watch and the setting of a few controls, the deed was quickly done.

The next morning, as my guard ended and Drummond's began, we proceeded as usual, moving inexorably towards the magical moment when the foot guards, drawn up inside the railings, pause to salute the horse guards, passing by on their way to Whitehall.

As the distant jangling and clattering drew closer and closer, announcing the imminent arrival of the cavalry, Drummond nerved himself for his big moment. And then, suddenly, they were there. He drew himself up to his full height, filled his lungs with air, opened his mouth and stopped dead.

He was unable to proceed for quite some while; even when muffled within the recesses of a bearskin helmet, a Bourne & Hollingsworth kitchen alarm-clock proved to have a gratifyingly long, loud peal.

My response to the Army's timely announcement that we were to be posted overseas was the traditional one of Information Officers everywhere: I reached for the atlas, the newspaper and the relevant volume of the *Encyclopaedia Britannica*. The British Cameroons turned out to be not a group of Caribbean islands, as I had originally supposed, but a small cocoa-growing country tucked up tight in the armpit of Africa. That topographically accurate description does little justice to the stupendous beauty of the scenery we found there; Kumba, our destination, lay in the remote central district, shadowed by a huge volcano and entirely surrounded by lush, tropical rain-forest. Visually it was a distinct contrast to our last tour of duty; it was also considerably more alarming.

The management of this hitherto largely neglected British colony seemed to be in the hands of a small number of plantation owners whose days were spent supine beneath mosquito-nets with only a bottle of Scotch for company; the natives, understandably perhaps, were more than a little restless. In response to popular demand, there was soon to be a plebiscite which would decide the future of the country, and our role (not entirely official, I suspect) was to keep the peace in the meantime.

Despite the Saunders-of-the-River overtones this was, at last, real soldiering; people could, and did, get shot. I was intensely excited by the entire experience, much more so than the average guardsman whose major concern, as always, was with his stomach. The efficiently-run French Cameroons to the south had fresh croissants and Camemberts flown in from Paris daily; we subsisted on emergency rations and avocado pears, a local staple that in most cases singularly failed to appeal. ('Effing sorbo rubber, sah!')

The natives, the first black men that many of us had seen, spoke pidgin English; luckily there were missionaries on hand to explain that, when a man wrote to us of having six children but no erection, he was complaining about his housing situation rather than his lack of virility. The missionaries had mastered not only the local language but also the local culture, of which the most fearsome aspect was the widespread belief in the power of the witchdoctor. Their small hospital had to cope with a steady stream of patients, many of them mysteriously ill with nothing other than the firm conviction that they were being cursed to death; they had been told that they would die on a certain date and, with only one or two exceptions, they did. Things improved considerably when a bright young medical

[ 67 ]

officer hit on a simple but highly-effective solution: hide all calendars and lie about the date.

One of the most disturbing discoveries I made was that the locals did indeed All Look The Same To Me (as no doubt we all did to them). Monday-Tuesday, the *dhobi wallah* that I suspected of being a terrorist agent, was dismissed (on a Wednesday) and replaced (on a Thursday) by a much more trustworthy gent of similar hue calling himself Alexander Wankah. It was, of course, the same man and he was not, of course, a terrorist; they, though everywhere in evidence, were nowhere to be seen.

The jungle surrounded us on every side; sentry duty suddenly made sense. When we left the base to go out on patrol we lay flat on the floor of the truck, hoping vainly to avoid detection, but news of our departure always arrived before us; our radio was no match for a highly-efficient jungle telegraph whose syncopation I admired without in any way understanding.

It was little better inside the compound; standing one morning under the pierced bucket that served us as a shower, naked and defenceless, I had no option but to stare helplessly in horror as a hand suddenly snaked out from behind a tree and made off with my watch.

I was increasingly anxious to get to grips with this apparently invisible enemy, and when a guardsman reported that he'd been offered a substantial sum for his rifle, I encouraged him to agree to a meeting that very evening. As he edged nervously into the middle of the moonlit clearing, armed with a hastily carved wooden replica, his unseen audience included myself and half-a-dozen enormous local policemen. Officially, it was their operation; I was there only as an observer. And, indeed, observe was all I could do when, as a shadowy figure finally materialised out of the darkness, they launched themselves precipitately into the fray. A great deal of yelling and screaming indicated that someone somewhere was on a hiding to nothing and, as the dust cleared, the victim was revealed: one very battered, very bruised guardsman. Of the rifle, and of the enemy, there was not a sign.

My paranoia evaporated almost overnight; there could be no denying that, this time, ninety-nine per cent of the population really were out to get me. Lying in my hammock, trying to ignore the cacophony of strange sounds that issued from the surrounding darkness, I began to face up to the issue that I'd been busily avoiding for nearly two years. Its epicentre lay three thousand miles away, a huge house set in a vast park: Shugborough.

My family's first link with the house, and the estate that surrounds it, dates back to the time of Elizabeth I. William Anson, a Lincoln's Inn barrister from Dunston in Staffordshire, bought himself an extensive acreage that had originally belonged to the Bishops of Lichfield, moved into its largest house and had a son, William, who had a son, William, who demolished the original house and began to rebuild on a much larger scale.

This third William had three children: a daughter, Jannette, and two sons, Thomas and George. Thomas, the heir, was artistically inclined, collecting pictures, patronising craftsmen and helping to found the Society of Dilettanti.

George, Thomas's younger brother, was a man of action; he joined the Navy and spent much of his early career on the South Carolina station, harrying the Spanish. An American society hostess, Mrs Hutchinson (who seems more than a little smitten), wrote of him: 'He has good sense, good nature, is polite and well-bred, free from troublesome ceremoniousness, generous without profusion, elegant without ostentation, and above all of a most tender, humane disposition.' That kind of testimonial ought to be enough for any man but George Anson was patently not content to be merely an all-round good egg: in 1740 he embarked on an epic four-year circumnavigation of the globe.

Its major purpose was to capture the huge Spanish treasure ship that carried the pillaged bounty of the New World back to the Old and, despite the ravages of storm and scurvy, Anson's much depleted squadron succeeded admirably in its task. Having almost incidentally saved the city of Canton from destruction by fire, George returned to Spithead in June 1744, where his rich cargo, the largest ever taken, required thirty-nine wagons to carry it up to London.

Later he was created Baron Soberton in recognition of a famous victory over the French off Cape Finisterre. Later still, as First Lord of the Admiralty, he introduced the series of reforms that earnt him the soubriquet 'The Father of the Modern Navy', a weighty responsibility that did not prevent him from putting to sea to lead the successful blockade of Brest two months after his sixty-first birthday. He was a bit of a hero of mine.

Thomas, meanwhile, was busying himself building an expensive town house at 15 St James's Square, whilst also completing his father's renovations at what was now known as Shugborough. George's substantial prize monies must have helped considerably, as did the fine china he kept bringing back from abroad; less so, perhaps, the other little trinkets he despatched which included a herd of wild goats from Corsica.

Despite having been described by Mrs Hutchinson as 'far from being a woman-hater', George, now Admiral Anson, married late, though well. His wife, the daughter of a Lord Chancellor, died childless in 1760 and he survived her by only two years. Thomas, now Member of Parliament for Lichfield but still a bachelor, inherited his brother's fortune (though not his title) and died in 1773.

Jannette had married one Sambrooke Adams, a country squire from Market Drayton, and their son (who was also, by some strange coincidence, called George) now inherited the estate, adopting the Anson name in the process, and marrying Mary Vernon (through whom, if I was so minded, I could trace my ancestry back to William the Conqueror). Their son, Thomas, continued the improvement of Shugborough, remodelling the house, extending the park, and marrying Anne, the artistically-talented daughter of the pioneering agriculturalist Thomas Coke of Norfolk. In 1806 he was created Viscount Anson, and when he died twelve years later the title passed to his son, another Thomas.

This 2nd Viscount, a friend of Fox and Greville, was created Earl of Lichfield in William IV's Coronation Honours and went on to become Postmaster General, presiding over the introduction of Rowland Hill's Penny Post. He had a racehorse that won the St Leger; Greville described him as 'liberal, hospitable, frank and gay, quick and intelligent'. It seems that the liberal hospitality often got the better of the quick intelligence, for in 1840 the entire contents of the house, with the sole exception of the family portraits, were auctioned off to pay his debts.

(His daughter Louisa was a woman whose lack of charm earnt her, too, a small place in history. At a house party in Ireland, Lady Louisa's younger fellow-guests, outraged by some act of petty-mindedness on her part, removed the name card from the door of her bedroom and replaced it on the door of the lavatory, a room which was always subsequently known as the Lady Lou, or, for short, loo.)

The 2nd Earl of Lichfield did what he could to restore Shugborough's fortunes, as did the 3rd Earl, who married another of the Norfolk Cokes, Lady Mildred.

By the middle of the twentieth century, the estate, growing steadily more independent under three hundred years of family management, had become both a self-supporting community and a thriving commercial concern. But its current figurehead, the 4th Earl, my grandfather, was now seventy-six and said to be sinking fast, despite having moved south to the healthier air of Bournemouth. The house, which my grandmother had carefully moth-balled and dust-sheeted before she left, stood empty; Liz and I lived in a small cottage at the other end of the estate.

We had always been, by and large, a long-lived family. I'd worked out that, in the normal course of events, I shouldn't be called upon to take over the title (6th Earl to my father's 5th) until somewhere around 1985. Wild oats long sown, I'd be in my mid-forties, almost certainly married and probably the father of several children. It was even possible that by then I might be quite looking forward to shouldering the responsibilities I'd be required to assume. Now, however, at twenty-one, the prospect of early promotion seemed distinctly unappealing.

Not that I had anything better in view. The Army had, as I'd originally suspected, turned out to be a pleasant enough way of passing some time; more than that, it had channelled my adolescent energies into positive action, providing some much needed self-confidence at a difficult age. But it didn't feel like a long-term relationship.

Even if I'd considered myself temperamentally suited to a career in one of the professions, it was now much too late. Given the length of time it took to become qualified, I'd be old and grey well before I saw any action as a doctor or a lawyer and, besides, academic study was still not my strong point.

The only things I knew I was good at were drumming, diving and boxing, none of which seemed to offer much by way of alternative careers. Prizefighting was right out; my confidence had been severely dented the previous day by a close encounter with a meatier-than-average guardsman cook called Harrison. ('Go on, Harry,' a voice cried when the bell went, 'mash him like yer does the spuds!' – and he did.)

It seemed as if I had little choice but to accept the inevitable with as good a grace as I could muster. It shouldn't be that difficult, surely. The estate more or less ran itself. All that would be required of me was the maintenance of dignity consonant with my new role as a major landowner.

That could be a problem; I'd already made an ass of myself at my first public appearance. The Shugborough tenants and employees had kindly hosted a ceremonial dinner to mark my coming of age, a rather strait-laced affair held amidst the stygian gloom of The Station Hotel, Stoke-on-Trent. After the dinner, and the toasts, and the exchanging of illuminated scrolls, I was expected to give a speech; I spent days sweating to encapsulate my protean views on the landlord–tenant relationship in a few pithy paragraphs only to be betrayed at the last minute when my nervously-fluttering hands let the precious notes fall to the floor. Bending to retrieve them, I hit my head on the table and knocked myself unconscious; 'My Lords, ladies and gentlemen' were the first and last words the assembled company heard from me for quite some time.

On the other hand, I'd been living in the city too much recently. If I could avoid being run off the estate as utterly unsuitable, the exchange of Levis for Harris Tweed would at least mean I'd get some regular fresh air.

That last home thought from abroad brought me up short. Fresh air was the last thing I wanted. The atmosphere I hankered after was thick enough to cut with a flick-knife, sin-tinged with the wail of saxophones, clotted with the smoke of cigarettes and worse: Real London.

Villiers, with his talent for the improbable, had produced one day, like a scruffy rabbit from a hat, an acquaintance of a cousin of a chum: Michael Beby, a man who proved to have enormous charm, dubious pedigree, high standards and low friends. He was hip, he was cool, he was my first beatnik, and together the two of us, Boswell and Johnson, Flanagan and Allan, Falstaff and Prince Hal, sallied out into the labyrinthine heart of jazz city.

The regular haunts, the Flamingo Club, the Two Is, Seymour Street and Pelham Crescent, were like a secret village, a sub-cultural inferno consisting of countless low-ceilinged low dives where we discussed Coleman Hawkins, John Coltrane and the essential problems of existence in one and the same breath, whilst keeping a constant eye open for the arrival of the plain-clothes policemen whose hobnail boots were always a dead giveaway despite the shades and drainpipes.

Beby's rich vein of cynicism was moderated only by a deeply held belief in the lasting value of girls, or, as he preferred to call them, 'chicks', and we pooled our resources to mutual advantage. The relationship that we established was otherwise based entirely on mutual bewilderment, each of us regarding the other as if he'd just arrived from another planet. I took his passport photographs and he wrote me poems, a habit I at first distrusted deeply but later grew to appreciate.

I resisted the temptation to show these poems round the Mess. 'Lord Anson wishes to read us some poetry.' I thought not. But I have them still:

Well then, one of my busy friends,
Will you learn today
That Money never ends,
And there really isn't any special law
That prevents the rich from dying
Just exactly like the poor.

I'm not qualified to judge their merits as poetry but I appreciated the sentiment; his was a realm that existed beyond mine, outside it, at an oblique angle to what the rest of the world thought of as Real Life, and exploring it in his company was as thrilling as going out of bounds. I lay in my hammock and tried to imagine myself explaining this to the tenant farmers; the prospect of the 5th Earl of Lichfield being swept up in a drugs raid on a dingy jazz cellar might not thrill their blood in quite the same way as it would mine. Beby, much to my regret, might have to go.

Running Shugborough, after all, was the job I'd been trained for, the post for which I'd been bred. It was my purpose in life. And anyway, ultimate argument, I had no choice: Noblesse Obliged. At least it wouldn't interfere with my real interest; I'd already worked out that my grandfather's dressing-room would make a palatial darkroom.

The gibbering shriek of monkeys and the chirruping of tree-frogs drowned a series of heartfelt sighs as I worried myself to sleep.

The dreadful Villiers was stationed at Bamenda, just fifty miles to the north-east. After fifteen bone-crunching hours in a Land Rover on some of the worst roads I've ever seen, we were reunited just in time to pay a call on the famous Fon of Bafut. The Fon, or ruler, owed his power to a genetic freak: his family were giants in a race of pygmies. The village was a doll's-house collection of tiny beehive huts clustered cosily round his, much larger, home where he kept a photograph of the Queen, torn from the *Illustrated London News* of 1953, and a large drum, which he insisted we play. After we'd told him how much we admired his photograph and he'd told us how he'd made the drum from the skin of a German officer 'slain in fight', he offered us the pick of his wives, all of whom were small but, following the custom of the country, beautifully marked. Only the tact of the platoon sergeant and the lust of the average guardsman finally ensured that honour was satisfied on all sides.

Returning to Kumba, I was immediately despatched to one of the up-country villages; a message had arrived in a forked stick, demanding that we send three regiments to defuse a rampaging elephant. The initial reaction of the village elders when I and my lone guardsman arrived was to complain bitterly that they had carefully specified three regiments and here were only two. We explained that our other regiment had a headache and couldn't come and then joined them in squatting on our haunches to watch an extremely wizened old man work an elaborate elephant-detection spell with an unsavoury collection of beans, bones and chicken feathers. Their position, he announced in due course, indicated that our quarry was directly ahead of us, a mile further on into the jungle. As we set out I distinctly heard an alarmingly manic trumpeting from behind me but, despite my protestations, we spent twelve fruitless hours searching the dense jungle, only to find, on our return, that their banana plantation had been trampled to the ground in our absence.

After a day or two, when we'd helped them to trap the huge beast in an equally huge pit, we were allowed to leave, bearing the tail as a kind of thank you present. Driving back down to the camp, the aroma of freshly-butchered pachyderm thick in my nostrils, I couldn't help but feel that there was a message in all this but, try as I might, I couldn't work out the parallels. I began instead to draft a telegram to Paris, asking my mother what she could find under E for Elephant's Tail in the *Larousse Gastronomique.*

# [6]

On 14th October 1962, at 2.30 in the afternoon, I walked out of Wellington Barracks for the last time; I was earning my living from photography within the hour.

Shortly after our return from Africa, the news that I'd been dreading had finally arrived; a telegram informed me that my grandfather was dead. When I asked for compassionate leave, the Army, with its customary brutal efficiency, allowed me precisely thirty-six hours in which to sort everything out; mortified, I immediately applied for permission to resign my commission, a lengthy process which took at least another year to work through the system.

In the meantime, as meeting followed meeting at the offices of the family lawyers, I began to see why that rogue elephant had seemed such an omen; the problems were everywhere where they were supposed not to be. The realisation that we now owed what amounted to a substantial sum of money didn't come as that much of a shock (I'd read enough romantic literature to appreciate that this was the traditional discovery of a young aristocrat); it was the nature of the liability that intrigued me. We were not, apparently, indebted to my grandfather's wine merchant, or his tailor, or even his bookmaker; we owed the money to Her Majesty's Government.

Patiently, the lawyers explained that my grandfather had, at some time in the recent past, made over a large portion of the estate to my father. It was, they went on, a wholly legitimate and extremely common manoeuvre whose main purpose was to avoid potentially punitive death duties. Regrettably, they concluded, nobody had been able to foresee that both men would die within two years of one another. We now had not one tax to pay but two.

In Bournemouth my ailing grandfather, physically in decline yet still in full possession of his mental faculties, had examined the looming problem from all sides and concluded that there was but one option: relinquish the house.

I found the idea curiously alarming. The house may not have held many happy memories for me but it was the closest thing I had to a home of my own, enshrining everything I'd been brought up to think of as my birthright and my heritage.

Beby's friends, whose alternative value system had little room for any of this, refused to sympathise; property is theft blah blah. The best defence I could manage at the time was the story of Admiral Anson's lion.

Anson's flagship, the *Centurion*, had undergone a comprehensive refit when it returned from its voyage round the world; the impressive figurehead, a richly-carved and painted lion, was declared surplus to requirements. George III gave it to the Duke of Richmond who, for reasons best known to himself, used it as a sign on a public house. Several years later, William IV, faintly put out perhaps, had retrieved the now rather dilapidated lion and presented it to the Greenwich Hospital. Later still, feeling its age, the figurehead fell to pieces and was carted away to be stored in a distant outhouse where it was discovered by some relation of ours and taken to Shugborough. The largest single remnant, the lion's left leg proudly mounted on a plaque, had been a familiar part of my childhood. Pickled in the salt of seven seas, worm-eaten and cracked with age, its only practical purpose was as firewood; I loved it not for its worth, which was nil, but for its value, which was beyond price. I felt the same way about the house; like it or hate it, the values it enshrined were part of my mental landscape.

Further lengthy meetings with the lawyers convinced me that my grandfather had been absolutely right; there really was no other practical solution. The estate, though prosperous enough, had few liquid assets; the profit had always been ploughed back into the land, almost literally so at times. The only other means of raising the cash, to dispose of a portion of the estate itself, would have required the sale of so many acres that the property would be reduced to little more than a large farm employing only a handful of people. Reluctantly I conceded: better the house than the estate. At least it would be in good hands.

The contents of the house, the furniture, the paintings and the fine china had all been bought specifically for Shugborough; had we now followed the example of the 1st Earl, and simply auctioned the lot, a distinctive collection would have been dispersed for ever. As to the house itself, few private individuals had the means to purchase it outright; the eventual owner would almost certainly have been either a Greek oil millionaire or a giant multi-national. I suspect it was my grandmother who suggested the only dignified alternative: Shugborough and most of its contents became the property of the nation.

The complex bartering required to effect this simple if bold solution involved offer and counter-offer, proposal and counter-proposal, and provided highly-gainful employment for flocks of lawyers for several years, but eventually a solution acceptable to all parties was hammered out: the Treasury wrote off our tax debt and Shugborough, together with most of its contents and the income from a small endowment, was given to the National Trust.

My feelings were predictably mixed, a disturbing compound of relief and regret. The house was a heavy responsibility; I had not been looking forward to the worry of funding comprehensive rewiring or a set of new roofs. I was also relieved not to have to find a way to live in the house; three hundred years of history had given it a distinct personality, a strong style of its own which I wasn't at all sure would suit me. One of us would have had to have changed and I had an uneasy feeling it would have been me.

But the way in which it had, or had not, reacted to the whim of each of its successive owners was an essential part of the house's history, the central dynamic that had kept it alive over the years. The National Trust, I knew, would be very careful not to impose any such demands, requiring only that Shugborough stand still and assume the placid dignity considered generally suitable to a historic monument. The house was about to be embalmed; it seemed a sad end to such an illustrious story.

Beby had been astonished to hear me say that all this had very little to do with personal income; I suspect he'd rather looked forward to helping me buy my first yacht. But I had never expected to become suddenly rich as a result of my grandfather's death; although I had now nominally inherited a substantial fortune, I also had a board of trustees to answer to, a body of profoundly sensible people whose purpose was to prevent my blowing the lot on fast women and slow horses. Their concern was with the estate's survival, not my personal happiness; I wouldn't starve but I certainly wouldn't be rich.

In fact, for the first few years my weekly allowance amounted to precisely £3 6s 11d. It was enough to keep body and soul in relatively close proximity but little more. Since I was patently not now required to bury myself in the country, I was going to have to find something else to do with my time; more to the point, if I was to avoid being answerable to the trustees for every move I made, I would have to find an independent source of income. I needed a job after all.

As my time in the Army neared its end, I spent more and more time avoiding the issue in the darkroom at Wilton Place. One morning, my attention drawn by a small commotion on the street below, I picked my way over the recumbent forms of several maiden aunts to peer out of the window, just in time to see two men, one pale and faintly dashing, the other considerably older and more frail, carrying in what looked, at first glance, like a vanload of assorted old iron. A second glance revealed that their cargo consisted mainly of battered metal boxes, complex tangles of electrical cable, and an assortment of emaciated aluminium lamp-stands. I recognised those lamp-stands from illustrations in photographic magazines: they were tungsten lights. I was down the stairs and introducing myself in approximately seven seconds.

The younger of the two men, Dmitri Kasterine, confirmed that, yes indeed, he and his partner, Michael Wallis, were professional photographers, that, yes, they had just taken a short lease on this, their first studio and that, no, they didn't need any help, thank you.

By dint of silently waiting poised behind the door, listening for one or other of them to leave or enter the building, I managed to bump into them quite often over the next few weeks, and when I discovered that only medical reasons had prevented Kasterine from joining the Grenadiers, I shamelessly grasped the opportunity to stretch our conversations further and further, first to their door, then into their hallway, and finally into the inner sanctum itself.

This first glimpse of a real studio proved instantly addictive and I found more and more reasons to just pop in whilst passing. As the depth of the gulf that yawned between my status as a keen amateur and their matter-of-fact professionalism became embarrassingly clear, I stopped trying to show off and learnt to sit in a corner, marvelling silently.

The first thing that I noticed was the size of their cameras; Kasterine patiently explained that whilst my relatively compact 35mm might do for snaps and reportage, anything else called for more detail and therefore larger film: half- or full-plate cameras for advertising and fashion work, the marginally more flexible 5x4 Speed Graphic for weddings. I also noticed that their modelling lamps stayed on for hours at a time and threw out an enormous amount of heat; Michael patiently explained that my tiny hand-held flash unit simply didn't provide enough power; tungsten was unwieldy but efficient.

As role models, they presented a keen divergence of possibility for the aspiring amateur: Wallis was charm personified, hiding an encyclopaedic knowledge of photographic technique behind an outward façade of dithering helplessness; Kasterine was his exact opposite, all vim and vigour, dash and drive. It seemed I had a choice between languid artistry on the one hand and frantic dedication on the other. I inclined towards the latter but tried to keep my options open.

Michael's forte, elaborate high-quality still-lives, was much in demand for advertising but, left to his own devices, I could see he would produce the world's most beautiful pictures four days too late, trying first this filter, then that, then this lighting set-up, then that. Dmitri's role was to keep up the pressure, pacing up and down with a scowl, attempting to head off Michael's frequent requests to take a break, either for ten minutes ('. . . a little sit-down, perhaps?'), or twenty ('. . . a little lie-down?').

Fashion was the responsibility of Dmitri, who had an extremely good eye for black and white work, especially portraiture. While Dmitri issued his instructions to the alarmingly self-confident models, Michael would do his best to look inconspicuous, floating around in the shadows beyond the lights, whence he would offer the occasional piece of highly-constructive criticism in a piercing whisper.

Every single moment I could spare was passed either in my darkroom or their studio. Upstairs, in the evenings, I spent hours arranging and re-arranging a complex array of (empty) bottles and glasses, learning to use my eyes, often without taking a single picture. Downstairs, I would have been quite happy just to sit and watch the two of them in action but I realised that would be to risk ruining our slight relationship by straining their patience; I made myself excessively useful instead, coiling cables, sweeping floors and producing endless cups of coffee.

It was early days for them, and I was fascinated to see people so preoccupied, not with art, or duty, but money; this was obviously a serious business. I began piecing together some basic biographical data.

Dmitri was not only the son of a White Russian emigré: he was, somewhere in what seemed like a different dimension, a prince (I promptly forgave him his occasional moodiness). His scarred face came from an early career as a racing driver; he had also, prior to meeting Michael, been a wine merchant, an insurance broker and an airline pilot.

Michael, apparently, came from a genteel background where he had always been considered something of a sickly child. Educated entirely at home, turned down for National Service, he had managed to escape officialdom almost entirely with the result that, even in late middle age, he drifted through life serenely untroubled by mundane considerations such as income tax. Despite his veneer of almost effeminate elegance, he was passionately interested in women, often going to extraordinary lengths in pursuit of a pretty face. (Mary Burr, who joined us as a secretary and soon became a close friend, always claimed to have met Michael in a Scientology class.)

A month or so passed and, since I hadn't yet been thrown out, I promoted myself to more specialised responsibilities: filing the negatives, cleaning the cameras and changing the burnt-out light-bulbs. Whenever the opportunity arose, and often when it didn't, I'd remark on how surprised I'd been to find that they didn't have a full-time assistant, count to ten under my breath, then mention casually that well, well, it was only four months to go before I left the Army.

Only four months, only three months, only two months, only one month; they began to exchange looks that spoke volumes whenever I opened my mouth. I gave it up as a lost cause and started thinking seriously about agricultural college. When the day of my departure finally dawned I considered celebrating my new-found freedom by splurging a week's allowance on a bottle of champagne, decided I wasn't convinced I'd done the right thing, and simply went straight back to the flat, slipping into the studio as usual. Still in uniform, I reached for the habitual broom, as Dmitri came over for a quiet word: 'Michael and I thought three guineas a week for four weeks and see how it goes. What do you think . . . ?' It seemed I had a job.

The three-year apprenticeship I served with them was certainly the most formative period of my life. Kasterine and Wallis influenced me in a thousand and one ways, not the least of which was their insistence that photography was not only worth doing, but worth doing well. Not that we took ourselves too seriously; they both had sharp senses of humour, particularly Michael, who thoroughly enjoyed being more than a little eccentric.

Smog was still a familiar part of the London landscape in those days and Michael, who remained much preoccupied with his health, took to wearing a surgical face-mask to go to the Post Office, terrifying the inhabitants of Knightsbridge by looming out of the shadows at them, waving his stick and humming Charlie Parker at full volume from behind his mask. Things went from bad to worse when he developed a new, improved method of smog filtration and began soaking his increasingly grubby mask in Dmitri's vodka. He'd inevitably return from his little walks drunk as a skunk on spirit fumes, with absolutely no idea of whether he'd posted the letters in a pillar-box or a litter-bin.

Dmitri, who was much more down to earth, had an almost obsessive desire to find out about the world in general, and photography in particular; his insistence on the highest possible standards impressed me enormously and we spent hours together poring over the work of acknowledged masters like Irving Penn and Richard Avedon, taking a magnifying glass to the models' eyes to search out the tell-tale reflections that revealed just how the lighting effects had been achieved.

He was a man of constant enthusiasms, some of which passed more quickly than others, including his institution of a swear-box that drove us to experiment briefly with technical terms as replacements for deleted expletives. Given the obsessional rigour with which he pounced on the smallest speck of dirt in the darkroom, I thought it Scheimpfluggingly fortunate for all of us that he never accompanied me on my regular trips to Balham, where our films were processed by an aged printer with seven cats, all of which habitually prowled around the kitchen table-top where he sat marking up our prints amidst the remains of last night's supper.

It's a long way from Knightsbridge to Balham, spiritually as well as geographically; in the early stages of my employment the journey was made easier by my sleek, second-hand E-type Jag. As time passed it seemed increasingly inappropriate to my tyro status, and when my godfather Sir Seymour Egerton quietly suggested that the first requirement of a professional was surely a sensible attitude to money, I saw his point and bought a bike for ten bob in the Harrow Road.

Once I'd mastered the art of balancing a launderette bag on the handlebars, the savings I made on petrol and laundry bills, when added to the fruits of an occasional illicit dip into the gas meter with a marmaladed knife, paid for my weekend railway ticket to Staffordshire where I was keen to be seen out and about on the estate. (I stayed well clear of the house though; my grandmother was in occupation there, sorting and annotating, packing and wrapping, clearing the ground for the National Trust.)

Whenever I could, I tried to save enough for two train fares: one for me and one for Wallis. Vast though the pleasure of his company undoubtedly was, this was not the main reason for my regularly repeated invitations; I'd discovered that one of the few places he could be guaranteed to remain undistracted for long enough to impart real wisdom was in the corner seat of a second-class railway carriage. Pulling down the blinds to reduce interference still further, I would sit opposite him with my Focal Encyclopedia, the photographers' bible, open on my knees whilst I interrogated him ruthlessly on the finer subtleties of Watkin's Factor and the Purkinje Shift.

To my eternal gratitude, and continuing astonishment, he was never once at a loss for a cogent explanation; his exposition of everything from shutter synchronisation to Scheimpflug's Condition (which turned out to be a relationship between intersecting planes of focus rather than a disease of sheep) was clear, concise and unremittingly deft. Years later, his talents as a teacher were finally displayed in front of a deserving audience when he was invited to lecture at the Royal College of Art. He taught me almost everything I know about photography; he also taught me about life. His death in the late Seventies was a blow from which I took a long time to recover.

I think the greatest thing he taught me was that a good photographer rarely, if ever, makes it up as he goes along. Photographs happen, not simply at the moment the shutter is released but for a long time afterwards (developing, printing, assessing, cropping, re-printing, re-assessing) and for a long time prior. Michael would spend days in crumpled thought before an important shoot, and once he'd made his mind up about something there was no shifting him. Useless to tell him that the fly he wanted in order to show the scale of some printed circuit was simply not available in the middle of winter; much easier by far to bicycle to London Zoo and spend hours in the Elephant House with a jam-jar.

(Once we had the fly back in the studio the problem, of course, was how to kill it. Moral qualms apart, we couldn't just swat it; the shot called for a three, not two, dimensional insect. The ever-handy bottle of vodka came in useful yet again; the fly buzzed round interminably before finally, and I like to think happily, crash-landing in the drink. We fished it out, dried it off with a hairdryer, and immortalised it on film where, alas, even in death it looked supremely drunk.)

The only faint regret about my new career was that it gave me much less time for my previously overcrowded social life. With the darkroom, the studio, and the endless bottles-and-glasses, I was lucky if I could afford the time to take a girl to dinner once a month. If I could afford the time, I could rarely afford the dinner and I evolved a number of strategies to cope with the problem of maximum dash on minimum cash. Having arrived at my girlfriend's house promptly on the dot of eight (hopefully remembering to remove bicycle clips before ringing doorbell), I would wait just long enough to drink a glass or two of her father's sherry before suggesting, as suavely as possible, that rather than trek into the West End (in an expensive cab), we might stroll (half a mile or so) round the corner to a little restaurant I'd discovered, quite by chance, just the other day (after a lengthy search through a guide to budget bistros).

Ensconced in a candle-lit corner booth, a rapid scan of the menu would quickly reveal the cheapest *hors d'oeuvres* on offer, for which I would declare a sudden and lasting passion (particularly easy if it was something with which I could credibly scoff at least half-a-dozen or so rolls). The conversation had then to be rapidly steered round to the subject of the enormous (and totally fictitious) lunch we'd had at the studio that day, a tactic that served a threefold purpose, distracting my guest's attention from the quality of the fare on offer, stressing the glamorous nature of my job, and preparing the ground for my studied refusal of a main course ('No, no, you go ahead, I couldn't eat a thing.'). The sight of women eating thrills me still.

My work, of course, was interesting, fulfilling and rewarding too, but rarely, if ever, glamorous. Lunch, on the other hand, and supper too, did occasionally materialise but only when we were working on a food shot.

One evening I was left alone in the studio darkroom to process some shots we'd taken that afternoon, a cascade of potato crisps caught tumbling appetisingly out of a bag. These were no ordinary crisps; Michael, despite my protestations of lengthy experience in stop-motion photography, had insisted that the only satisfactory way of achieving the desired effect was, as ever, to fake it, hanging each carefully arranged crisp from a length of near-invisible fishing line. Since the average crisp seemed to shatter at the very thought of a length of fishing line, we decided to fake the scale too, and persuaded the manufacturer to bake, at great cost in time and trouble, a special batch of giant poppadom-sized versions, twelve inches across.

And very nutritious they were too. I scoffed the lot, whilst the film was in the fixer, only to find that we'd entirely omitted a vitally important filter and that the whole thing would have to be done again.

This time the haul-up I so richly deserved was postponed indefinitely; we were far too busy poring over the rough sketch we'd been sent for our first major press ad: a hymn to steak-and-kidney pudding.

Wallis, once bitten, made sure we ordered two giant steamed

puddings, one of which was put to warm in the oven whilst the other became the centre of the attentions of two photographers, one assistant, one art director, two account executives and a client. The session went extremely well, Michael had only one short sit-down, the deadline was only slightly broken, and the test shots showed that they were some of the best pictures we'd ever made: time for dinner. As the satisfied professionals disappeared restaurant-wards round one corner, a crowd of hungry amateurs, alerted by my telephone call, swept into view round the other, brandishing knives, forks, spoons, plates and a daffodil that someone had whipped from a window-box.

When we'd settled ourselves down, laid the table and given the daffodil, at least, a drink, the moment came when I found myself, serving-spoon poised over steaming pudding, savouring the conviviality of the occasion and wondering, not without a minor pang of apprehension, what the trustees would make of this, my alternative apotheosis.

I plunged the spoon into the pudding and the air was instantly filled with the damp aroma of steamed paper handkerchiefs, several dozen of which were all that the pastry crust contained. I had learnt another valuable lesson; the camera concerns itself only with externals.

# [ 7 ]

One of my relations, hearing of my new job, delivered a crushing and all too predictable verdict: 'Far worse than being an interior decorator; only marginally better than hairdressing.' Today, familiar with the rugged charms of professional cameramen like Bailey, Donovan and McCullin, such snobbery seems laughable but in the mid-Sixties, when 'youth culture' was still struggling to be born, ignorance of photography was the rule rather than the exception. What little knowledge there was was usually built on the slender evidence provided by infrequent visits to a portrait studio, an embarrassing occasion at best, all too often made even more uncomfortable by the fawning attentions of the self-styled Society Photographer. ('Poodle-fakers!')

Thanks to my experience with Wallis and Kasterine, I now knew better: photography, particularly commercial photography, was a hard, cut-throat business, where survival demanded boundless inner reserves of discipline, energy and drive. I found it thoroughly bracing and my family's consistent refusal to take it seriously only added to my determination to succeed.

My mother, insulated from my day-to-day struggles by the width of the Channel, remained strictly neutral on the subject, hastening neither to encourage nor condemn. The trustees' attitude was equally opaque. Not without a vestige of my old paranoia, I decided they were giving me just enough rope to, if not hang, then at least severely strangle myself, a self-inflicted wound that I presumed would be swiftly followed by a quick twitch of the purse strings, intended to bring me back to heel before I dragged the family name further beyond the pale. If I wanted to be truly independent, it was clear that I would have to measure my success, not just on my terms, but on theirs as well. I had to make money.

Michael and Dmitri, confident that I offered no meaningful competition to their now thriving business (and quite possibly bored to tears with my relentlessly cheerful presence in the studio), had always encouraged me to go out and get work of my own. Initially, at least, it was hard to come by.

My first few jobs continued the paid-portrait theme that had begun at Harrow; I now charted my fellow-pupils' further progress with a series of shots celebrating engagements, marriages and christenings (usually but not always in that order). My fee was a flat five guineas, take it or leave it, no-mate's-rates-I've- got- a- living- to- earn- and- a- bunch- of- trustees- to- win-over; an essentially boorish attitude that probably lost me a lot of friends.

I also, for a fee, took photographs of their children and to my surprise soon developed a small but valuable word-of-mouth reputation. Perhaps, not having grown up in the company of toddlers, it was my insistence on treating children as nothing other than small adults that made it work, or perhaps it was simply my insistence on photographing them as naturally as possible, ideally outside rather than in the studio. Whatever the reasons, the children and I generally formed, fairly easily and fairly rapidly, relatively straightforward relationships, certainly more straightforward than between myself and their young mothers, who when confronted with a tradesman tended towards a frigid politeness which sometimes melted rather too suddenly when they discovered that I was, in fact, quite house-trained.

I learnt a great deal about the photography of children from the work of two other first-class photographers, one a close friend, Dmitri, and another less so (though growing closer now that we were very distantly related by marriage) – Tony Snowdon.

Both of these worthies, had they known, would, I'm sure, have been more than a little sniffy about my first commercial job, some advertising shots for a product which called itself The Linea Thermal Relaxer Belt but which looked suspiciously like a man's corset. The shots I took of Pinky and Perky, the two semi-naked, deeply beefy male models, appeared in small ads all over the country ('Gentlemen, a word about your waist-line . . .'). Luckily there was no byline.

My first officially-credited picture appeared on the Hickey page of the *Daily Express*, attached to a photograph of an elegant girlfriend of Brian Alexander called Madeleine Rampling, whose picture I'd taken outside Harrods holding her rather tedious little dog. I can still remember standing in the pouring rain in Fleet Street at midnight staring at the paper and revelling in the thought that hundreds, no thousands, no millions of people would soon be able to see the new name I'd chosen for myself: Patrick Lichfield.

Rather than waste my hard-earned fees on the often exorbitant cost of professional fashion models, I started to make enquiries amongst friends and acquaintances and, before long, my tra-ditional little black book slowly began to fill with the names and numbers of willing girlfriends, girlfriends' girlfriends, and girlfriends' girlfriends' girlfriends, leavened here and there with a welcome sprinkling of aspiring actresses, amongst them Madel-eine Rampling's cousin Charlotte and an extremely nice, polite but rather prim girl called Joanna Lumley.

The doyen of fashion photography was John French, a man who displayed a consistently amazing ability to come up with shot after shot that was fresh, original and full of impact. Dmitri pointed out that he had another, less obvious but even more valuable, attribute: he always maintained the perfect balance of emphasis between the model (the excuse for the shot) and the frock (the purpose of the shot). Newspapers seemed to carry a lot more fashion then but the standards of reproduction were usually appalling (as I had cause to know; after some pictures I took of her appeared in the *Express*, a very hale Lady Docker wrote me an anguished letter claiming to have been inundated with messages of sympathy for her obvious ill health). Despite the limitations of the medium, John French's shots were always clean and bright and sharp; it had to be something to do with both his lighting and his printing. I spent hours practising on an increasingly battered piece of Persian Lamb, a dark, dense fur that was reputed to be the most difficult thing in the world to photograph clearly; I never matched that French polish.

The experience came in handy, nonetheless, as did the little black book, when an extraordinary fake fur company called Astraka employed me for what was (unbeknown to them) my first proper fashion job. With the invaluable assistance of my little hand-picked team of dedicated amateurs (which included Jacqueline Bisset, a shy but extraordinarily attractive girl, whom one of my flatmates met on a bus), the pictures turned out quite well and seemed to keep the client happy. I knew though, sooner or later, I'd have to face up to the challenge of The Real Thing.

My first Proper Professional came heavily recommended for her intelligence and looks alike, and she proved more than amply blessed in both departments, accepting my tentative suggestions with what struck me as extraordinarily good grace and then adding a few ideas of her own which made her a total joy to work with. (Her name is Grace Coddington and she went on to become Fashion Director on *Vogue*.)

Flushed with self-confidence and convinced that all models were equally bright, I chose my next two girls purely on the basis of their size and shape. When I greeted them at the door, they dropped their she-said-to-him-so-he-said-to-her conversation just long enough to acknowledge my presence before picking it up again to continue across the threshold, along the corridor and into the dressing-room ('Look, I said . . .'). Fifteen minutes later, as they strolled on to the studio floor, it was still in full spate ('So, anyway, she said . . .'). I coughed nervously and there was a brief moment of blessed silence whilst I prepared to explain what I was looking for.

The first girl indicated her readiness by removing the gum from her mouth and then turned to her partner.

'Wottya think, Sharon? 'S a fifty-seven innit?' she said, assuming a pose like a pregnant stork.

'Nah,' said Sharon, leaning forward, pouting and grabbing her left shoulder with her right hand, 'thirty-nine.'

'Erm . . . ,' I said.

'We could do six?' (A French chambermaid)

'Or seventy-six even.' (Joan of Arc)

'Wottya think?' Dumbstruck, I realised they were asking me.

'No, no, no,' I said, furiously multiplying my birthday by my shoe size and dividing by three, 'I think it's more of a twenty-three, don't you?'

'Oh, twenty-three!' they chorused and struck poses that made them look surprisingly human, whereupon things went fairly smoothly for the rest of the session.

My worst fears confirmed, I decided to go back to basic portraiture and give fashion a rest for a while. In the seven or so years that had passed since I first accompanied Liz to her coming-out balls my social life, indeed my entire life, had undergone a total metamorphosis. My new friends, a loosely-knit group of students, actresses, musicians and media people struck me as utterly fascinating but I knew the only photographs of them that Fleet Street would pay me for would be reportage shots that showed them either taking drugs, or having illegitimate babies, or plotting the downfall of the state (and pregnant anarchist junkies seemed in rather short supply).

What the papers really wanted was debs, hundreds of them, preferably photographed having a jolly nice time dancing the night away at some high-society party. I dusted down my dinner jacket, stuck a couple of spare rolls of film in the pocket, and headed off to Berkeley Square.

Mixing with my former class-mates again, seeing them *en masse* and *en fête* for the first time in so many years, proved to be a thoroughly disturbing experience. Few, if any, of them knew the first thing about photography and once they'd screamed and giggled a bit at the occasional flash ('Say cheese, Johnny!' 'Fromage! Har, har.') they paid me no attention whatsoever as I prowled around the outskirts of their pleasure, picking off likely targets. This kind of informal picture-taking (pioneered in the Fifties by Anthony Armstrong-Jones) was still a fairly new idea in Fleet Street and the picture editors were reluctant to give up the formal, and often heavily retouched, pearls-and-teeth pictures that they were used to, so I also carried one of the studio's Rolleiflexes, which when fitted with a flash gun made me look remarkably like a divorce detective. ('I say, you're not actually going to show anyone that picture of Camilla and me, are you? Cause a frightful fuss, har, har.')

I thought that the big camera had a tendency to make people look like dummies and I much preferred the smaller 35mm which seemed to have the reverse effect, particularly when used with available light (Dmitri had shown me how to uprate HPS to an astonishing 800 ASA). Few of either sort of picture got published but eventually I managed to negotiate a contract with the *Express* (twelve shots a year at fifteen quid a head) where a surprisingly benign journalist called Robin Esser and his picture editor Frank Spooner almost made it all worthwhile by regularly taking me out to a real restaurant for a real lunch (in the course of which I would often mystify them by having at least two *hors d'oeuvres*).

It didn't take me long to realise that Spooner and Esser were less interested in my technique than my ability to put accurate names to the faces I was photographing, a comparatively rare and potentially valuable asset on which I cashed in unmercifully.

I also did a bit of deb-spotting for the *Sunday Mirror* where Brian Clifford and Derek Jameson once suggested I should go off and photograph this namesake of mine, the Earl of Lichfield, reputedly a bit of a man about town. ('Oh no, ghastly fellow, totally worthless,' I said, leaning closer over the table. 'Bit of a poodle-faker.')

*Queen*, which had been bought by a young, ebullient and highly ambitious Old Etonian called Jocelyn Stevens and was getting an increasingly good reputation, had kept its society page, 'Jennifer's Diary', virtually untouched despite the radical changes elsewhere in the magazine. Betty Kenward ('Jennifer'), having apparently begun to notice my children's photographs on pianos here and there, now began to use them for an occasional spread. The money from those, plus the *Sunday Mirror*, plus the *Daily Express*, persuaded me it was time to bid the bike farewell. The trendy little yellow Mini Cooper which replaced it was considerably faster but not half as much fun to drive; it did, however, allow me to extend my ambivalent attentions to the *jeunesse dorée* of the entire Home Counties.

The price I paid for these continued breaches of yet another unwritten code was social exile. The hostesses were as keen as I was to see their parties in the paper but that didn't mean they had to be nice to me, and they weren't, placing me decisively below the salt and beneath notice, inevitably seated, if seated at all, behind a pillar opposite a place laid for a guest who never came. In five short years I'd sunk from being a Deb's Delight

Annunziata Asquith and I set off for a Burberry shoot. On the extreme
left and extreme right are my beared assistants, Chalky and Pedro

Under the Burberry umbrella with Annunziata Asquith

Joanna Lumley and I with our Havannas

Model Pauline Stone and I go our separate ways

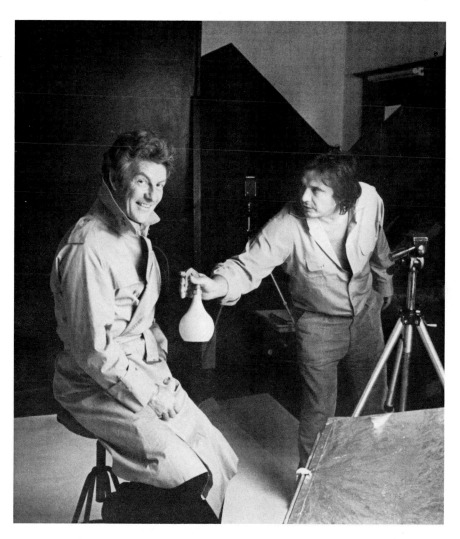

David Bailey at work with me

With a little photographic equipment at Aubrey Walk

Burberry work. Behind me is Chalky Whyte

Me by Chalky and Pedro

The author, Helmut Newton, David Bailey

Preparing to photograph Princess Margaret

Awaiting the arrival of Prince Charles and Princess Diana from St Paul's Cathedral in 1981

Preparing the group. Her Majesty is standing back to take her own view

My own wedding day

My daughter Rose                    My daughter Eloise

David Bailey photographs father and son

(even if Not Safe in Taxis) to a total pariah; I blushed all the way to the bank.

As an antidote for this over-rich fare, I spent a day or two photographing down-and-outs at a hostel in Poplar. The meths-drinkers were akin to the champagne-drinkers inasmuch as they either abused me or ignored me but the smell of urine that permeated the place was a distinct contrast to the Belgravian gardenias. It was all something of an eye-opener.

Perhaps the biggest job I had in 1964 was my first overseas assignment: pictures, for the *Daily Express*, of Princess Anne-Marie of Denmark, shortly to be married to King Constantine of Greece. (The fact that my mother was now Princess Anne of Denmark may, or may not, have had something to do with this commission. I suspect not; the *Express* was rarely that subtle.)

Having been up all night covering a deb dance in Scotland and having snatched considerably less than forty winks on a bench at Edinburgh airport, I was not entirely match-fit when I arrived at the Danish summer palace of Fredensborg. My confidence was not increased by the knowledge that an upset at the laundry had left me wearing, not my best bib and tucker, but my second best, the one with no right sleeve. (When the elbows went on my shirts, I used to rip off the entire arm; the cuffs were retained in place with a strategic cuff link.)

Very nervous, very hot and very, very early, I followed a footman down an immensely long corridor, telling myself it would soon be over, only to find myself shut up for two long hours in a magnificent but rather stuffy ante-room, unable to do any reconnaissance, unable to find the lavatory, unable to do anything but review all the hundred and one things that could and therefore would go wrong. By the time I was finally released to walk behind another footman down another mile or so of corridor, I was a shambling ruin.

The Queen was in the drawing-room having tea with her

husband, King Frederik, and their three daughters. After we'd all been introduced, Queen Ingrid placed in my quivering hands a cup that was filled entirely to the brim. Surface tension contested nervous tension for what seemed a small eternity until the King, anxious for his carpets, stepped in and removed my teacup to the safety of a nearby side-table. Inviting me to sit down, he told me to relax, and suggested I take my jacket off.

Without thinking, I did as he suggested, thereby revealing a large stretch of bare arm, naked as nature intended and garnished with a small tattoo. Above the thunder of blood rushing to my ears I thought I heard the King saying something that sounded remarkably like, '. . . Mr Birchet in the Waterloo Road?' and looked up to see him pulling up his sleeves and undoing his shirt to display what is undoubtedly one of the most impressive collections of tattoos I have ever seen; King Frederik, a naval man of long standing, was something of a connoisseur.

Anything that happened after that was bound to be an anticlimax but the pictures, masses and masses of them taken at great speed over the next two days, proved rather successful and appeared all over the world. I had learnt another lesson: I work well under pressure.

Back in London, I resumed my vampire existence, locked up in the studio darkroom from breakfast till dinner-time, emerging under cover of darkness to rush off to capture the high life of Cheltenham or Tunbridge Wells, then locking myself back in my own darkroom to develop the prints. That is the only excuse I can offer for my lamentable failure to notice that, all around me, the Sixties had finally begun.

The Sixties, of course, began in 1960; 'the Sixties', a much more thrilling affair, didn't really begin until 1963, and the Profumo Affair. Or 1964 and the first Labour Government for thirteen years. Or 1965 and MBEs for the Beatles. Or, the favourite by a short head, 1966 and *Time* magazine's cover story on 'Swinging London'.

Whichever it was, it was slow to get off the ground and certainly subtle enough to pass right over my head; I was too busy doing my own thing, an occupation that I only later realised was the quintessentially Sixties pastime. But eventually even I began to notice that Something was Going On. Where it was going on, and when, and what precisely it was, were not so easy to discover; the Sixties, it seemed, was more of a mood than a movement.

It was the best of times; it was the worst of times: affluent, frivolous, permissive, radical, naïve, degenerate, self-indulgent, hedonistic, anarchistic, wild, wacky and totally way out, it was also highly confusing especially for the media (a Sixties invention if ever there was one).

Finding themselves faced with what seemed to be nothing other than lively chaos, the journalists decided to deal with it in the time-honoured way by concentrating on personalities; the gossip columns, and then the feature pages, and then even the headlines themselves were slowly taken over by a small and consistently shifting set of movers and shakers ('the in-crowd') whose every thought and every action was chronicled with a reverent solemnity that now seems deeply silly. The names on the list seemed to change almost as often as the views they expressed – but then again, change, they told us, was what it was all about.

There certainly seemed to be some kind of change in the air, especially where attitudes to class were concerned, although again it was difficult to pin down what these changes were. As my grandfather had perhaps sensed, post-Suez, post-empire, the old idea of the aristocratic ruling-class had suffered a severe and probably fatal blow; there was little place for hunting, shooting and fishing types in a world of hovercraft, jet engines and nuclear power stations. The reaction against the peerage was symbolised by Viscount Stansgate's decision to drop his title in order to pursue his career as plain Anthony Wedgwood Benn; I toyed with the idea of renouncing my title for approximately five minutes, decided that now I could afford to eat in restaurants I might as well get a good table when I wanted one, and settled down to watch the show.

Star billing appeared to be reserved for working-class-boys (-and-girls)-made-good; I began to garner an occasional mention as a kind of make-weight thrown in to balance the scales: the upper-class-boy-gone-bad. My trustees, I imagine, hated every minute of it; I enjoyed it immensely.

Claims to represent the new, iconoclastic, thrusting values of the younger generation were soon being made by representatives of every trade, vocation and profession known to man, from prelates to prostitutes and from civil engineers to sagger-makers' bottom-knockers, but some jobs were undoubtedly perceived as being more trendy than others.

Fashion was very definitely with-it, particularly if it was sold from a 'boutique' (a word that used to imply all kinds of excitement but has now sadly dwindled to summon up nothing more exciting than gift shops on ocean liners). With talented designers like Mary Quant and Barbara Hulanicki setting the pace, some very odd clothes indeed began to appear in the studio as I edged cautiously back into fashion photography; we did our best to evolve some equally strange ways of photographing them. (Once I had nerved myself to talk to, rather than at, the models I found them an invaluable source of ideas, usually other people's; I owe Barry Lategan, in particular, a substantial debt for the use of his crossed-Sellotape-as-soft-focus-filter idea as well as his practice of processing Kodak Royal X Pan film in paper developer to produce grain-like lumps of porridge.) The real trick, however, was to find models whose personalities were strong enough to keep up with the clothes, Jean Shrimpton and Twiggy being the two most consistently conspicuous examples, along with Pauline Stone and Sandra Paul.

Pop-music was even more where-its-at; I found myself photographing a group called Gerry and the Pacemakers and a girl called Priscilla White (who posed quite happily on a camel on Clapham Common and promptly turned into Cilla Black).

As the decade progressed, it became clear that the one thing that united pop-stars, politicians and pundits was a preoccupation with Image. Suddenly the word was everywhere, and image-makers edged to the front in the popularity stakes. David Bailey, Terence Donovan and Terry Duffy, their working-class accents no handicap, were up there at the front, alongside Tony Snowdon who'd somehow managed to attain both the New and the Old Aristocracy in a few short years. The rest of us were close behind, waving frantically. The rules, with which I did my best to conform, were made clear right from the start: we were expected to appear, as often as possible, as publicly as possible, in really strange clothes and with at least two stunningly beautiful blondes on each arm. Come early, stay late, don't punch the newspapermen. If we were rash enough to want to take pictures during all this, the subject on which our lenses should be trained was equally clear: ourselves.

'David Bailey's Box of Pin Ups', designed by Mark Boxer, was a particularly high-profile case in point, thirty-six wonderfully cold, hard portraits of photographers, actors, designers and pop people, staring out at the world in all their unretouched reality. As the habit of people-spotting spread, the (often genuine) achievements of the New Aristocracy paled into insignificance against the mountain of trivia that built up beside them, detailing their likes, their dislikes, their taste in food and their size in socks. With the active connivance of their interviewees, these personality profiles began to irretrievably smudge the previously clean line between public and private. Gossip became news, and there were no secrets, a fundamental change of attitude which rippled right up to the doors of Buckingham Palace which opened, at the end of the decade, to admit television cameras intent on following the Royal Family's every move, both at work and at play.

For all this heady talk, the first truly famous person I actually photographed (on, I recall, 22nd May 1965) was a distinct disappointment – Zsa Zsa Gabor. The only time she could spare me was whilst she was having her hair done, but I worked fast, got the shots, and tore home to develop them in time to present them for her approval first thing next morning. She promptly tore up twenty-one of the twenty-two prints and was very rude about the one that remained; for some people, it seemed, re-touching would never be out of fashion.

When I found myself in a house-party that included Edward Heath, I photographed him too, standing on a distant cliff looking meaningfully out to where the Europe he was leading us into loomed. He, too, turned out to be not unaware of Image; although the picture showed him only as a distant speck, dwarfed by the noble landscape all around him, he refused me permission to use the pictures because he'd changed his spectacle-frames.

New York's *Status* magazine (whose name says more about it than I ever can) began commissioning me to take photographs of London's great and good, a flexible definition that turned out to include Michael Fish (the trendy tailor whose clothes I was just beginning to be able to wear and who turned out to be no relation whatsoever to my governess) and Michael Caine (whose bachelor flat off the Bayswater Road impressed me with numerous clues to his life-style: the stocking left draped across the chair, the lipsticked cigarette butts and the lingering smell of scent were still in exactly the same places when I went back several days later for a retake).

Anxious to break away from the increasingly surreal world of dancing debs, I touted my small portfolio of celebrity portraits all over London, and when I met a man who knew a man who knew someone who had a bit of influence at Time-Life, I arduously pursued the trail to its logical conclusion and won, after much nodding and smiling, a valuable commission. *Life* magazine, then still a major force in photo-journalism, was doing a series on what they called The Great Families of Yurp; I drew the card marked Blenheim/Churchill/Marlborough.

It was a prestigious job that intrigued me for several reasons. Blenheim had been open to the public since 1950 and, as it seemed increasingly likely that I might soon move into my own small flat at Shugborough, I was anxious to pick up a few hints on what it was like to live with a constant stream of visitors. I was also genuinely interested to see how one of the last truly noble English families was bearing up under the onslaught of the Swinging Sixties. I was also looking forward to a nice lunch.

It was not the first time we'd met; Serena Russell, one of the Duke's many grandchildren, had been a girlfriend of mine whilst I was still in the Guards and, when it was decided to throw one of the grandest balls since before the war, I was lucky enough to be invited to stay the weekend.

The guest-list for the ball ran to nearly two thousand people but the house party was a much more select affair, and I was extremely annoyed with myself when I got held up in the holiday traffic. When I finally skidded to a halt on the gravel only half-an-hour before dinner, I lost no time requesting a hovering supernumerary to take my luggage up to my room whilst I found, and apologised to, the Duke. A quick inspection revealed that my fellow-guests had not yet come down, so I continued up to my room where I found my bags, not yet unpacked, unceremoniously dumped in the middle of the floor. Puzzled by this departure from Blenheim's notoriously high standards, I struggled with my studs and just made it in time to join the now assembled company in the Drawing Room and introduce myself. The Duke, who could be a formidable man when crossed, seemed a little gruff but not irreparably put out and proceeded to introduce me to the guest of honour.

'I don't think you know the American Ambassador, Mr Whitney?' But I did. I'd handed him my bags not ten minutes ago, convinced he was the butler. He gave me a pleasant smile, shook my hand and, professional diplomat that he was, never referred to the incident again.

My return to Blenheim, as a considerably less callow youth and an accredited representative of the world's media to boot, ought, I thought, to be comparatively plain-sailing. It was nothing of the kind. The Duke, whose temper had not mellowed with the passing years, showed absolutely no memory of me whatsoever, looked daggers when I enquired after the health of his grand-daughter, posed for a few very stiff shots, and made it quite clear that, as a tradesman, I was expected to find my own lunch.

My brief, as I reminded myself over a burger in a Wimpy Bar in nearby Oxford, was to capture The Great Family, not merely The Great Man and, luckily, the rest of the Spencer-Churchills proved to be totally charming. I took some super pictures, including one showing the younger grandchildren in the room where Churchill was born and another of the Duke's heir, the Marquess of Blandford, inspecting his livestock. *Life* complimented me on my handling of the assignment, selected the pictures they wanted, and left me to submit the rest for syndication.

A few months later, the phone rang in the early hours of the morning.

'What are you?' demanded a faintly familiar and extremely angry voice.

'Patrick Lichfield.'

'No, you're not, you're a shit!'

It was Lord Blandford, absolutely incensed that a photograph of him, winningly captioned 'Informal custodian of ten thousand acres, Lord Blandford with pigs', had appeared in that morning's *Express* without his permission.

Even I had to admit that the picture, taken out of context, did look a touch satirical. Nonetheless, as I attempted to explain, that was not my intention. Nor ought I to be held responsible for the choice of photograph, pulled from a file by an assistant picture editor. And anyway I thought it was rather a nice picture. Didn't he think that promises to haul me up in front of the Press Council were a little excessive? Apparently not; the telephone went dead.

I spent a very worrying couple of days seeing blood-curdling visions of a promising career cut off in its prime. Repeated phone calls attempting to apologise met with nothing but a refusal to speak to me. The friends who rang to pass on news of his lordship's latest threats didn't help matters much by rubbing salt in the wound with recollections of his wedding to Mrs Tina Onassis ruined by a sudden invasion of press photographers.

It was my mother who eventually came to the rescue. Reconciled, it seemed, to having a scapegrace son, she rang the only other photographer she'd ever met, Tony Snowdon, who rang the wiliest man he knew, Jocelyn Stevens, who spoke to the injured party, Lord Blandford. Wearing my best suit and a shirt that I made sure had two sleeves, I was summoned to the Marquess's impressive City office where I proceeded to wear out his carpet with my knees. He accepted my apology, withdrew his complaint and we went on, slowly, to become quite good friends.

There was a price to be paid for this rescue operation. Rashly and in the heat of the moment, desperate to save my career, I'd made large promises all over the place. Shrewdly, Jocelyn decided to cash one of them in. I was appalled to find I'd condemned myself to spend a considerable time working for *Queen* at rock-bottom rates. Photographing debs. ('I say, Johnny, do look, it's that man with the camera again!')

# [ 8 ]

Back in Berkeley Square, there'd been changes. The girls' dresses were shorter, the men's hair was longer, dance bands were giving way to disc jockeys and I even saw one man in a kaftan rather than a cummerbund. Beneath these cosmetic alterations, however, the world of the debutante remained staunchly the same and just as dispiriting as before; my only small delight was watching Betty Kenward (Jennifer of 'Jennifer's Diary') in action, gathering information with the practised ease of an industrious queen bee masquerading as a social butterfly.

The unposed 'candid' photograph had almost become the rule rather than the exception whilst I had been away and my quarry, who sometimes seemed to know more about the rules of the chase than I, now went to elaborate lengths not to notice me whilst somehow always managing to maintain a best-side-towards-the-camera profile. ('Young man,' hissed a duchess after I'd snatched what I considered a particularly telling shot, 'I wasn't ready!') I comforted myself with the thought that, this time at least, I was working for *Queen*.

Jocelyn Stevens, nephew of press baron Sir Edward Hulton, had inherited a vast sum of money when he was just thirteen days old; he'd treated himself to *Queen*, a hitherto respectable society paper, as a twenty-fourth birthday present and turned it almost immediately inside out. Ably assisted by Mark Boxer and Anthony Armstrong-Jones (both of whom had been at Cambridge with him), Jocelyn rapidly established the magazine as the keenest arbiter of all that was excellent in Sixties fashion. *Queen* remained a 'society' paper, of course, but now it was Jocelyn and his team who defined the term, updating the concept to include anything and everything they approved of and savagely excluding the rest, a policy that earned plaudits from everywhere, not least from the legendary Diana Vreeland, whose smile or frown could make or break fashion empires and whose American *Vogue* had become the yardstick by which all other magazines were judged. History does not record Mrs Vreeland's verdict on our debutante coverage but, sadly for me, it continued to be a feature and I continued to do it.

The flash-and-grab work with which I occupied my evenings was dull, but it was at least uncomplicated; not so the endless golden weddings, engagements and comings-of-age shots which, at fifteen guineas a time, occupied an important part of the rest of my day.

The discovery that these private portrait clients were usually even more frightened of me that I was of them had astonished me to begin with; it wasn't as if they had to do anything, after all, other than just stand there. Here again, I was failing to make allowance for the 'media factor'. Some of the more 'artistic' photographers, cornered by journalists desperate for several column inches of meaningful thoughts, had developed a distressing tendency to spout increasingly complex nonsense, much of it centring on the camera's 'ability to perceive' the 'real true inner essence of personality'. The camera, they said (having never had to photograph a tissue-filled steak-and-kidney pudding), cannot lie. I devoutly wished they'd keep quiet; my private clients were beginning to arrive at the studio doubly tense at the prospect of finally discovering 'who they *really* were'.

Things improved slightly when I began to insist on making as many appointments as possible in the late afternoon; the sun could then be declared close enough to the yardarm to justify the offer of a few stiff drinks. The tactic did nothing to improve my increasingly louche reputation but it settled the nerves admirably, for photographer and photographed alike. (It didn't always work. Certain of the more laid-back members of the Chelsea set tended to arrive having ingested more than a few nerve tonics of their own; one large vodka was often all that was needed to send them from cosmic relaxation into total catatonia.)

Having learnt my lesson with the professional models, I now made a point of talking to my sitters rather than at them, a tactic which they often found so surprising that they relaxed enough to produce good pictures. (Thanks, again, to the media, most of them expected to be the objects of an aggressively monosyllabic harangue: 'Yeh, that's great, hold that, smile, good, God my head, left hand down a bit, look angry, yes, good, now a happy happy smile, happy I said, get us an aspirin love, good, hold that, no, more teeth, yes, look up into the light, now down again, lovely.' It wasn't that I distrusted this technique; it simply seemed much too much like hard work. Taking photographs was difficult enough without having to talk about it all the time.)

It was easier with the 'celebrities' (another unfortunate coinage from the Sixties); they, at least, tended to arrive carrying a well-defined image, honed and polished over the years into something with which, presumably, they were fairly happy. If the worst came to the worst and nothing much else emerged, I could always settle for visually encapsulating the label rather than the personality: Sir Francis Chichester, 'weather beaten old salt', Bernard Braden, 'penetrating, witty, and sardonic', Susannah York, 'noble beauty', Dudley Moore, 'lovable clown', and so on.

Others proved less straightforward: how, when photographing Roger Moore, was I supposed to show an actor acting; how, with racing driver Stirling Moss, could I encapsulate courage; and how, given my deepening awareness of her wide-ranging

[ 109 ]

talents, was I to picture Joanna Lumley? (The answer seems to have been to put her in a bathing costume in the Serpentine in mid-March, a pose which demonstrated her professional fortitude if nothing else.)

The whole thing became much more complicated when dealing with 'ordinary' people, particularly when they showed such a marked reluctance to reveal their 'inner essence' on demand. I could usually make an educated guess at what kind of person they were, but turning that three-dimensional idea into a two-dimensional image was rarely simple. And I wasn't entirely convinced I had the right to make those decisions on their behalf anyway. It was all getting just a little bit complicated; sometimes I wished I'd stayed with the bottles and glasses.

This uncharacteristic spell of *angst* was only partly a sign of the times; most of it was the same old problem; avoiding the issue. This time the issue was simple, direct and extremely alarming: Wilton Place was scheduled for demolition.

Having discussed the issue at length, all of us had agreed it was time we went our separate ways. The entertainers of maiden aunts were beginning to drift away already, to America, the City and, in one case I suspected, the S.A.S.; Michael and Dmitri would soon be following them. I had to find not just a flat but, if I were serious about this photography business, a studio as well.

And that meant I had to earn some big money, quickly. The obvious answer, to try to persuade Jocelyn to pay me an at least half-way decent fee for the deb work, was simply not possible. He was notoriously tight about money; requests for a living wage were all too liable to detonate the famous temper which had, so rumour had it, already precipitated chairs, typewriters and even secretaries through his office window. I was desperate but I wasn't that desperate. And, although I hated, detested and loathed the idea of photographing even one more deb, I knew that *Queen* was a place where enormous changes sometimes happened overnight. If I could just hang on for another two or three months, there was a chance, a slim chance but a chance nonetheless, that something good might come of it.

The next day, Jocelyn called me into his office and asked me if I could be in the Caribbean the week after next. I hummed and hahed, consulted my blank diary, re-scheduled imaginary appointments in my head for all of three seconds and agreed that, yes, I probably could be in the West Indies the week after next.

Deeply gratified as I was by this Cinderella-like reversal of my fortunes, I still had my doubts. In the nature of *Queen*'s attitude towards life in general, and photography in particular, these assignments would be the closest I'd yet come to photo-journalism. And that, too, worried me.

My tenuous experience with various famous faces was journal-ism of a sort, of course, reporting back not only on the physical appearance of celebrities but also, ideally, on what they were 'like'. (Lacking any ideas on how to photograph the Grand Duke and Duchess of Luxembourg with a pomp and grandeur suitable to their title, I'd shown them simply going about their 'ordinary' lives, an approach that seemed to work quite well and which I hoped to develop further.) And the photographs I took in Holland at Princess Beatrix's wedding, despite the studied informality of the occasion, were presumably at least a little journalistic in flavour, given the nature of the event.

Unlike most photo-journalism, however, these jobs had been by invitation. The Von Thyssen wedding, to which I was very much not invited, had been rather different. (The young journal-ist with whom I was working, one Nigel Dempster, locked me in the boot of the bridal limousine and lost the key; when the bride and groom found me at their honeymoon retreat they were so astonished they agreed to pose for what turned out to be some quite good pictures.)

[ 111 ]

Photo-journalism was also, as I knew to my cost, much more competitive; photographing the Chaplin family at the première of the *The Countess from Hong Kong*, I'd lost an entire roll of film when, as I later discovered, the photographer next to me put his hand over the bottom lens of my Rolleiflex.

Working as a photo-journalist would be difficult; working as a photo-journalist from *Queen* would be even more so. Having defined the nature of the challenge, I was disappointed to discover that, on this trip at least, in-depth-photo-probe-scoop-exclusives were out. The feature was to be promotional rather than critical and all John Pringle (the dynamic young head of the Jamaican Tourist Board) really wanted in return for our flight, bed and board were some nice, big, bright shots that testified to the island's unrivalled atmosphere.

I nodded sagely and resolved to take a large pinch of salt; I was more than a little cynical about promotional work. As I packed my battered suitcase I resolved, above all, not to be lured into the travel brochure clichés: the palm-fringed ivory beaches, the tall fruit-stuffed cocktails, the happy, smiling black faces.

From the very first moment that the aeroplane doors were opened and the fuselage filled with the warm, wet smell of the real Jamaica, I was overwhelmed. In less than an hour, as a genuinely cheerful black face served me a huge and delicious fruit-stuffed cocktail at my table overlooking the most beautiful palm-fringed beach I'd ever seen, any doubts I had about photo-journalism or, indeed, 'inner essences', 'deep meanings' and even 'the nature of existence' vanished on the flower-scented breeze. Everything was visible, on show and crying out to be photographed, a rich and utterly exhilarating environment that threw up direct and potent images at every turn. The exuberant flamboyance of the scenery and the relaxed self-confidence of the people showed my self-consciously intellectual agonising up for what it was: mere masochism. I relaxed and prepared to take good pictures.

The quality of light alone gave me palpitations. When I photographed King Olav in darkest Norway, I was alarmed to find there were less than two hours of natural light a day; it was already obvious that out here the problem would be exactly the opposite, too much light rather than too little, especially the noon-day sun which swallowed everything in its glare.

The Jamaica trip was my first real chance to work in colour and I leapt at the opportunity, cracking off roll after vivid roll, exploring the island from end to end with the invaluable aid of Pringle's henchman, Winston Stonor, whose fascinating face proved an invaluable testing ground for my early attempts at finding the right exposure equation for dark skin. I did us both a disservice at first by opening up by as much as a whole stop, washing out the highlights and bleaching him back to pale fawn. It seemed that I wasn't the only person on the island having problems with skin tone; one elderly couple told me to leave my 'boy' on the porch, which made me very angry indeed. I took their picture nonetheless, with a wide-angle lens from a distance of about sixteen inches. Perhaps I might get the hang of photo-journalism after all.

The photographs and the stories went down well in London, as did the substantial amounts of revenue that came with them, generated by my dangerously charming accomplice on the island, advertising salesperson Ann Wace. I had to fight Jocelyn almost hand to hand to get my expenses, but that was par for the course.

A month or so later, as I was walking down Bond Street on a grey rainy day, my spirits were lifted by the sudden sight of my picture of the Jamaican Prime Minister's wife beaming out from a bookstall in full and glorious colour. I tried to imagine Edward Heath in a similar pose, brandishing a banana, and grinned. It was my first cover shot.

I was even more delighted to be sent back again less than two months later, when Jocelyn decided to do a proper feature on the island. This time, I was to be accompanied by a proper journalist, an American called Bradshaw to whom, in a typically *Queen*-like arrangement, I was supposed to introduce myself at the airport in time for the first flight out.

Early to bed in order early to rise, I was disappointed at having to miss the opening-night party at Nick Clarke's new restaurant, The Place Opposite. But I comforted myself with the thought that, knowing Nick, the festivities would still be under way when I passed by next morning on the way to the airport; Nick did a good breakfast. The last few bedraggled couples were, indeed, falling into the Fulham Road as I arrived at dawn, but there were still a few eggs left and I was soon seated at one of the tables tucking in.

My digestion was disturbed by a groan from one of the darker corners where, on closer investigation, I found a crumpled man in a crumpled suit trying to drown himself in a plate of ham and eggs.

'Morning,' I said, thinking, for no good reason, of the Officers' Mess.

'Mmnaargh,' he replied.

'Everything OK?'

'Nnnur!'

'Are you all right?'

'Nergh.'

'What's the matter?'

'Chrissakes? Got. Go. Airport. Meet. Twit. Called. Lichfield,' he enunciated very clearly, in an unmistakably American accent, and buried himself deeper in his breakfast.

'Ah,' I said.

I wiped him down, dragged him on to the plane and, almost as soon as we took off, fell asleep. An hour later, when I awoke, he'd disappeared. I found him in first class, to which he'd been upgraded following his announcement that he was the Earl of Lichfield. I was delighted to see that at least one person had benefited from my decision not to renounce the title.

Bradshaw crowned the first twenty-four hours of our acquaintance by confiding, the moment he set eyes on her, that he was in love with Anne Wace, which upset me a little as I had been contemplating a little adventure in that direction myself. Six months later, they were married.

Despite this unpromising beginning, our relationship bloomed and we did a good job of work together, analysing (and experiencing) as many of the island's pleasures as we could in the short time available to us. Faced with a brief to concentrate on the people I did just that, setting about it in a thoroughly systematic way by making out a list of every category of humanity on the island and arranging to record representative selections of them in a sort of photographic census. This rather desperate attempt to cut an enormous brief into bite-sized pieces became, after a day or two, a thoroughly enjoyable exercise and I began to get a taste for the challenges of handling groups.

We completed our work in record time, well in advance of our deadline, and, when Bradshaw suggested we retire to the other end of the island for forty-eight hours' deep relaxation before returning to London, I was happy to agree.

Somewhere along the bumpy road from Kingston to Montego Bay, the tin box that contained every roll of every film we'd shot that week went missing. I spent the next two days scouring each square inch of our route, asking everybody I met if they'd seen it, putting ads in all the newspapers, and generally creating an enormous commotion. With no film, there would be no pictures; no pictures, no feature; no feature, no future. The blood-curdling visions returned, made infinitely more moving by the growing conviction that the career that was about to be ended had, at last, actually begun to show signs of beginning.

The box was returned to us, in almost pristine condition, just three hours before our plane left. This time, at least, luck seemed to be running my way.

Indeed it was. Back from Jamaica and still basking in the after-glow, I was invited one evening for a drink at Lady Antonia Fraser's house in Holland Park. It was summer and the Bayswater Road, bathed in the evening sunshine, was like one long montage of Swinging London, girls in thigh-high P.V.C. miniskirts with Union Jack carrier bags, men with shoulder-length hair wearing crushed velvet trousers, and boutiques everywhere, all of them apparently playing the same track from the same LP: 'We Can Work It Out'. (Everbody who was anybody had an interest of some sort in a boutique; mine was in Annacat in South Kensington, started by two of my old girlfriends, Maggie Keswick and Janet Lyle.) As the cab sped westward into the setting sun, I turned my mind to the outstanding problem: accommodation, professional and domestic.

Fulfilling a none-too-secret dream, I was shortly to move back into Shugborough, where the small southern wing had now been officially declared surplus to requirements. But there was no way I'd be able to live there full-time and still maintain any kind of career as a photographer, none at all; I had to have a London base. Not only that, but I was also quite obviously going to need a studio, again in London, and ideally about a thousand square feet. If I continued to work for *Queen* for, say, another twelve months and if I could increase the private portrait work by, say, twenty per cent, I should just about be able to maintain a reasonable social life. If I could find a few other famous faces to photograph on my own account, say one or two a week, and if Tom Blau at Camera Press could make good his promise to sell the syndication rights, I should, repeat should, be able to afford the rent on a bed-sitting room or even a small one-bedroom flat.

On the other hand, of course, the famous faces might well have to be travelled to, which meant airline tickets, hotel rooms and other expenses, all of which I'd have to pay for myself. So perhaps it would be better to have something in reserve, just in case, and anyway I was going to have to buy quite a lot of expensive equipment when the bulldozers finally forced me out of Wilton Place, especially if I wanted to go over to those big Balcar studio flash units. But then again, if it was a choice of a studio or a flat. . . .

'FOR SALE, One bedroom studio.' The cabdriver, detouring through the leafy heights of Holland Park, was rattling along Aubrey Walk, a narrow street of small upright houses facing a reservoir. I yelled at him to stop, paid the fare, told him to keep the change, changed my mind and asked for a shilling to pay my bus fare home and walked back, as casually as a burglar, to peer in through the windows of the tiny three-storey house.

Kitchen on the ground floor, by the look of it, for which read darkroom and small kitchen (I didn't intend to do much entertaining), studio on the first floor presumably (nowhere near a thousand feet but maybe I could learn to live with that), and a tiny bedroom on the top floor. It was ideal. I had to have it. There was only one option. . . .

I walked round to Lady Antonia's in a thoughtful frame of mind. As far as I could tell, the trustees' attitude had mellowed considerably in the last year or so. They had given me a great deal of rope and I had yet, as far as they knew anyway, to come anywhere near hanging myself. They might still be some way from approving of my career but they were running short of excuses to actively disapprove of it. If I took the bull by the horns and approached them, as one might approach a bank

[ 117 ]

manager, with a carefully worded, carefully costed business plan, an invitation to invest some of my money in my future, maybe, just maybe. . . . Property was always a good investment after all. And surely nobody could fail to see I was successful, or at least becoming successful, or showing some signs of becoming successful quite soon, or might, sooner or later. . . . That bit would need careful phrasing.

Six weeks later, after a series of hints about how welcoming America might be to an impoverished young English aristocrat, I moved into Aubrey Walk.

It was like growing up all over again. From this moment on I was committed to making a substantial and continuous living from photography; it was the first step down the ever steepening slope towards becoming a commercial concern. Rather than spoil the new ship for a ha'porth of tar, I hired my first assistant, Liz Ramsay, whom I'd met at what was now my aunt's house at Fettercairn, who turned out to be a tower of strength, providing endless moral support, typing all the invoices and generally putting up with being worked to the bone for the traditional pittance (slightly more than a ha'porth but not much). She was also, as she needed to be, a talented photographer in her own right, as was her eventual successor, Berry (for Berinthia) Berenson, whose elder sister Marisa had been one of my earliest models. (Berry was a splendid darkroom technician who married the actor Tony Perkins, two patently unconnected facts that always struck me as being in some manner obscurely related.)

We christened the studio with a number of group shots for *Queen*, each one another small step towards Jocelyn's goal of producing a definitive list of the nation's trendies. I enjoyed this work very much, wondering with increasing delight who on earth he would find for me to photograph next. The working titles on the briefing memo were usually the first hint as to what was in store: 'Britain's best conversationalists' promised, and produced, a valuable fund of after-dinner stories; 'The ten funniest men in England' was a bit of a disappointment.

As Jocelyn's ambition grew, the size of the groups grew with it and, before long, we were almost batch-processing the in-people, cramming upwards of twenty people into the studio at a time. As the nature of the bond that connected the members of these groups became increasingly tenuous, more and more of the people who arrived at the studio turned out not to know each other and I found myself in the enviable position of playing host to a series of highly convivial gatherings of the bright and the beautiful.

On one occasion the guest list managed to be both extensive and exclusive: Lady Anne Tennant, the Bishop of London, Joan Plowright, Graham Hill, Eduardo Paolozzi, the Marquess of Bath, Charles Clore, Cecil Beaton, the Marquess of Queensberry, Mario but not Franco, Anthony Burgess, Ronnie Corbett, Osbert Lancaster, John Mortimer, Reginald Maudling, Jonathan Miller, Freddy Ayer, Sir Roy Harrod and an up-and-coming interior designer named David Mlinaric. It was apparent we were going to have a whale of a time almost as soon as the first of them arrived and, before too long, we were all relaxed enough in each other's company to make it an extremely pleasant occasion. (The crates of champagne Jocelyn had provided helped considerably.)

If I had any lingering doubts about 'inner essences' or any of the rest of that nonsense, this kind of job would have stifled them at birth. The technical challenge was enormous and, in most cases, left very little room for artistry. (Some people managed both; I'd been up all the previous night poring over some of Irving Penn's group shots in the latest issue of *Vogue*.) Much of the success or failure of this kind of work depended on basic organisation, persuading each individual into a position where he or she would fit neatly, but not too neatly, into a unifying composition.

Once the people had been cajoled into their places, the next problem was to get them to stop talking, a particularly challenging task on this occasion but one which was finally accomplished without too much bloodshed.

Finally, and most difficult of all, there was the task of producing a simultaneous smile from one side of the frame to the other, a difficult aim in pursuit of which I was quite prepared to fall off the ladder if required. As it turned out, no such tactic was necessary and we shot ten rolls of film before it was time to start shooing them out prior to the arrival of the next party.

Any kind of list of 'in-people' defines, by implication, a similarly exhaustive list of 'out-people'. The thought of actually photographing these shadowy figures no doubt occurred to many people at the time, but nobody dared to attempt it. Nobody except Jocelyn that is (with more than a little help from Nigel Dempster). Prompt on the dot of six, the studio filled with a motley crew: Billy Walker, David Jacobs, Godfrey Winn, Geoffrey Keating, Robert Pitman, Anthony Blond, Egon Ronay (or Eggon Toast as he was known around the *Queen* offices), Robin Douglas-Home, Robert Maxwell, George Wigg, Cyril Lord, Sir Cyril Osborne, the Earl of Kimberley, Justin de Villeneuve (Justin Newtown), Sir William Piggot-Brown, Mary Whitehouse, and Brigid Brophy (Bradshaw's head was touched in afterwards, at Jocelyn's express command).

There could not have been a greater contrast. The atmosphere was steeped in suspicion and unconvivial to a degree. We'd opened only one bottle of champagne and shot a mere half a roll of film when Robert Maxwell, who'd been regarding his fellow sitters with an increasingly beady eye, suddenly strode out of the room, followed pretty rapidly by the rest of them. It didn't matter; I had the pictures I wanted.

The working title for the double-page spread on which the two opposing camps were duly featured had originally been 'nice and nasty' but this was eventually discarded in favour of the somewhat more diplomatic rubric 'You can tell a man by the company he keeps. . . .' A much more honest description would have been, 'Quite a few people Jocelyn Stevens likes the look of, and quite a few he doesn't.'

With work like this, the very occasional commission from *Vogue* and a great deal more that was much less interesting, the studio was, before long, almost paying for itself (although there were still some months that were terrifyingly dead). Liz Ramsay seemed quite happy to be spending more and more of her time on administration in the office downstairs (booking models, arranging schedules, paying invoices and generally keeping the place going) so I hired an additional assistant, Johnny Encombe, a gentle giant whose studies at Oxford had been terminated somewhat earlier than usual after an unfortunate incident with a rifle, a college deer, and a late-night barbecue.

Encombe had one distinct advantage over Ramsay; when he let himself quietly out of the studio at dawn, having finished a long stint in the darkroom, nobody ever mistook him for a girlfriend.

I was beginning to pay the price for all those entrances into restaurants with blondes on each arm; the popular press, having attached themselves to me like a large and rather stupid stray dog, refused to be shaken off. Every so often I would open the door in search of milk for my morning coffee to find my blurred field of vision filled with damp mackintosh. For a while I pretended to ignore these attentions, but when one too many intimate dinners threatened to end in fisticuffs I did what I should have done months earlier and asked my erstwhile colleagues on the William Hickey column for their advice. 'Always answer questions politely, always issue denials firmly, and if you value your privacy make alternative arrangements,' they said.

It worked, but not as well as I'd have liked. Deprived of even the faintest foundation of fact for a story, the press retired to the nearby pub and embarked on epic feats of imagination on the back of beer mats. My particular favourite was a gallery of beautiful women ranged beneath the winning headline 'All lovely, all loved and all lost by Lord Lichfield.' I knew two or three of these women by sight; most of them, to my lasting regret, remain strangers to me to this day.

My mother (now returned to London, and wholly supportive of my career)was more than a little disturbed by all this and she appointed herself my unofficial press secretary, waking me regularly with an early-morning telephone call that detailed the latest outrage, quizzing me on its contents and then invariably concluding with a solemn promise not to talk to me for two, three or, in really bad cases, four days.

On one memorable occasion, her message was short and succinct. 'I am now, officially, as of this moment, not speaking to you for one month,' she said and rang off.

The only thing I could think of that was even remotely questionable was the most recent group portrait I'd done for *Queen*, intended to illustrate some fairly foolish Valentine's Day article on 'The thirteen most eligible men in England.' I went through the list of a dozen or so names in my head (Gerald Ward, Lord Lyle, the Aga Khan, Michael Pearson . . .), failed to find anything objectionable, counted them again and got twelve names rather than thirteen, went downstairs and checked in the job book, started sweating, got dressed, ran out to the newsagents, bought the magazine, turned to the appropriate page and discovered that, yes indeed, I was the thirteenth man. Worse, far worse, lurked over the page: my services as an escort were being offered as a prize in the accompanying contest ('Win a millionaire, after that it's up to you . . .'). Just one of Jocelyn's little jokes.

Several weeks later, despite my protestations, I found myself scheduled to have dinner with a lady named, inauspiciously, Venetia. Determined to express at least some independence in this ridiculous charade, I made a point of not changing out of my Levis and T-shirt, and opened the door to find a woman dressed to the nines and beyond in a little black dress, court shoes, and a chignon. We made stilted conversation for half an hour or so before leaving to dine, at her suggestion, at the Mirabelle, where an extremely expensive meal was ruined by yet more vacuous chatter leading, inevitably, to the overwhelming question, Do you think I'd make a good model?

My family's changing attitudes can, perhaps, be charted by the only good thing to have come out of all this, a poem sent to me by one of my less aged aunts:

How was dinner for two with Venetia?
Was she 'U' or just plain 'pleased-ter-meetcher'?
There'll be photos, I trust, of that fabulous bust,
And no doubt the rest of the cretia.

Is she dumb or just trying to fletia?
Is she chaste or just ends up benetia?
But take auntly advice, be she ever so nice
If she clings, you must promptly reletia . . .

Jocelyn, whose sense of humour was beginning to grate on me just a little, laughed like a hyena and then queried the bill.

Although the press, by some immense stroke of luck, seemed to have missed this particular outing, I was still subjected to enough attention to relish the thought of the seclusion that Shugborough would shortly provide. Real London was begin-

[ 123 ]

ning to pall, and the countryside that had meant so much to me as a child was exercising an increasingly magnetic attraction. But before I could even begin to reacquaint myself with all that, I had to come to terms with the house itself.

As my sister and I stood looking out over the park, we both, I think, shared a reluctance to turn and pass through what used to be the servants' entrance into the new quarters that awaited us. Here in the south wing most of the rooms, many of them familiar since childhood, were considerably smaller than those in the rest of the house. They were easier to heat and furnish but still very pleasantly proportioned. With little or no interference from my grandmother (who had now retired to Devon) and an enormous amount of highly practical input from Liz, a long series of meetings with the National Trust had finally resulted in agreement on which rooms seemed to go together to form the most harmonious accommodation.

The old second dining-room, with its impressive book cases, would become our main dining-room; my old bedroom, a breakfast-room, conveniently situated next door to the new kitchen in what had been Liz's bedroom. My grandfather's dressing-room, which I'd originally marked down as a palatial darkroom, would now be a small sitting-room. (If I really wanted a darkroom up here, we could no doubt carve one out of a cellar somewhere.)

I had had time to get used to the idea that these rooms would not look as they had before; I knew that my grandfather's 365 razors would each have been carefully taken down from the dressing-room wall and added to the growing pile of domestic impedimenta that was soon to be auctioned. The rooms we were about to inspect would, I knew, be bare, comfortless and more than a little worn at the edges; I was not expecting a warm welcome.

To my surprise, we both reacted very positively; the spirit of the house was stronger than mere decorative contingency. Moving slowly through each room, measuring and planning, I began to see the rich possibilities of the place. By the end of the afternoon, we were already planning our first house-party. I was coming home.

The several months that David Mlinaric required to execute his bold (but attractively inexpensive) plans for the redecoration looked like being a deeply frustrating time for both of us. Liz, I think, was looking forward just as much as I was to the prospect of being able to entertain our friends out of the steely gaze of our elders and betters; she'd already seen one boyfriend's cuff-links confiscated to stop him carrying her off to Gretna Green. Her current admirer, Hugh Myddelton, was a nice man who had also known Miss G. and when I found myself sharing a pigeon hide with him in the middle of Scotland one cold morning I was only faintly amazed to hear myself agreeing, given I had a particularly empty month coming up at the studio, that I'd be delighted to join him on an overland trek to the Middle East.

My mother, to everyone's surprise, thought the jaunt a very good idea and proposed to make the whole thing more challenging by making a simple bet, which we accepted. Hugh's experience in the Coldstream Guards and mine in the Grenadiers proved extremely useful as we set about equipping ourselves with a Mini-moke (which looked reassuringly like something real travellers used despite being little more than a Mini with only minimal bodywork), a rather posh bell tent, several water cans, one camera body, one lens and a bottle of whisky.

On our first night, on the north coast of France, it took us two and a half hours to pitch camp and cook dinner; six weeks and several countries later we were in bed, having eaten, within fourteen minutes of arriving.

Hugh being Hugh, we couldn't just head for Nepal, or Afghanistan, or any of the other hippy havens that were beginning to be so popular with our contemporaries; we had to follow the footsteps of Alexander the Great. After France and Switzerland (where we had a meal with Villiers, newly arrived) and Venice and Trieste (where I looked up at the stars one night and realised our tent had been stolen), we spent a great deal of time in Yugoslavia, trying to find out where precisely Alexander went, before heading into Syria and Jordan, only to be stopped at the far border by rumours of an epidemic.

We had the inevitable row (something to do with a camel as I recall), we stole a great many vegetables from farmers' fields and we got some extremely funny looks at customs posts but we won the bet with my mother; petrol aside, we spent no more than £25 and, throughout the entire trip, neither of us once went indoors.

The pictures I took, very plain, no frills, pleased me enormously but the biggest lesson I learnt was at the hands of the tribesman who confronted us down the barrel of a rifle stuck through our tent flap one morning. As we emerged, hands held lightly in the air, I noticed that both Hugh and I were each, following our instincts, wearing nothing but a very wide grin. It was the first time I had evidence of how disarming a smile can be.

The knowledge was to prove very useful when, on my return, Jocelyn promptly despatched me with a journalist called Anne Leslie to do a feature on the Bahamas.

# [9]

Jocelyn's luck was extraordinary. The house in the Bahamas that he'd originally bought for a song turned out to be right in the middle of the proposed thousand-acre site of the Lyford Cay Club, a luxury haven for the very rich to whose facilities Jocelyn obtained access by making constant threats to erect a pornographic monument on his lawn. Anne Leslie and I enjoyed staying there very much especially when, shortly after we'd arrived, we fell over a major exclusive about potential Mafia involvement in the island's gambling industry.

It was real photo-journalism; we dodged about for several days, recording off-the-record conversations on tape-recorders hidden in Anne's handbag and sneaking pictures with a camera hidden under my arm. ('Young man,' hissed the gangster after I'd snatched what I considered a particularly telling shot, 'I'll break every bone in your body.')

After a week or so of this, Jocelyn himself flew in, intent not so much on protecting us as preserving his own sanity, now seriously under threat from the pressures and perils of Fleet Street, where he was beginning to be entangled in some highly complex machinations. Sensing an opportunity to revenge myself for *l'affaire* Venetia, I found a way to fake an urgent telegram from London which arrived at the house only minutes after he did and which demanded his immediate return. Although I'd fully intended to see the hoax through to the bitter end, I eventually relented and explained all just as we got to the emigration desk; he had difficulty seeing the funny side.

A few days later, claiming to have important people arriving any minute, he threw us out of the house. At the British Colonial Hotel, the newsworthy status of his guests was confirmed by the sudden omnipresence of sun-baked mackintosh. Princess Margaret and Lord Snowdon were a hot story.

Although I had met both of them before (and admired the sensitivity of the one and the professionalism of the other), this was the first time I'd appreciated quite how daunting it must be to live such a public life. Sensing the possibility of creating yet another episode in what they'd managed to make a very long-running saga, the world's newspapermen and photo-journalists were gathering in force, swooping and chattering all over the island like starlings at dusk.

The halcyon days we spent relaxing within the protective custody of Jocelyn's property reminded me of my time in the Cameroons; there were eyes everywhere, all of them focused on a small house-party which contained, ironically enough, not only the royal couple but also an embryo press baron with growing interests in Fleet Street and a young photographer hungry for work.

The paradox was clear to everybody, not least to the Snowdons who had an extremely ambivalent attitude towards being pictured together. Although they had no particular objection to being photographed either separately or in tandem, they were under-standably wary of being seen to do anything that might imply their approval of the press' interest in their affairs.

Whoever it was that broke into my hotel room and carefully exposed all the film I'd taken so far plainly credited me with a great deal more cold-blooded professionalism than I actually possessed; the only pictures I lost were some uncontroversial shots of the street-life of Nassau.

[ 128 ]

With two of my children, Thomas and Rose

A father with his son

A prolific author . . . and book signer

With David Bailey's wife, Marie Helvin

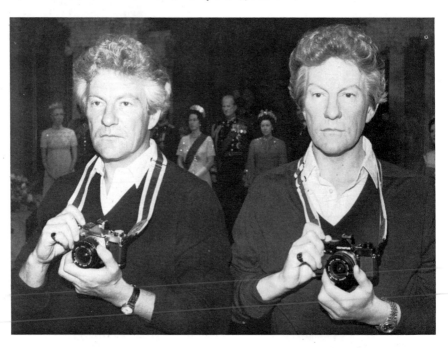

Madame Tussaud's asked me to pose beside my wax effigy

Photographing pork pies

A session with Yuki, the fashion designer and Dar the hairdresser.
On the right is Clayton Howard, essential to any Unipart shoot

With Jilly Cooper, Arizona 1985, for the Unipart shoot

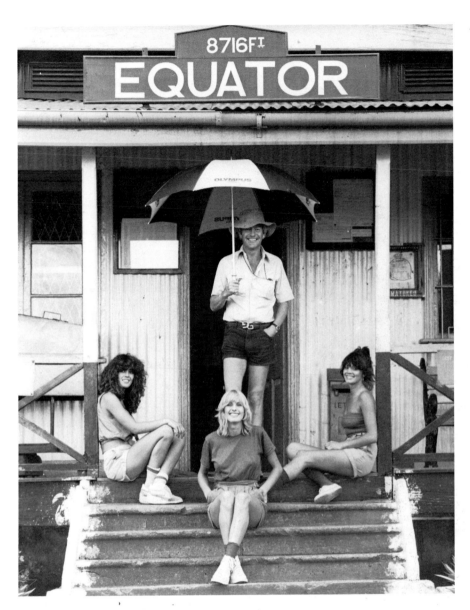

The record of another Unipart shoot, which is self-explanatory

A day out at Shugborough with mentally-handicapped children

We reached, eventually, a largely unspoken agreement: whilst I could not, and did not, expect Princess Margaret and her husband to actually pose for me, I was free (within certain strictly but silently defined limits) to take 'candid' shots of the two of them enjoying their holiday. It was plain, right from the start, that some activities were more acceptable than others; the problem was discovering what these were. Time after time my unfailingly jocular suggestions as to amusing, entertaining, and almost incidentally photogenic pastimes were gently dismissed with a stifled yawn (walking?), a fleeting frown (motorcycling?) or, at worst, a slight shudder (sunbathing? Hardly).

Jocelyn, eager for exclusives yet loyal to his guests, found it all particularly wearing; I grew all too familiar with the low, menacing rumble made by the gnashing of his teeth, an alarming noise that ceased only when, on the last afternoon, Tony suddenly suggested a little water-ski-ing and Princess Margaret, after a pause that seemed to last for ever, agreed.

In less than an hour, with the sound of the motorboat's revving engine already beginning to drift across the bay, I was safely concealed at the very end of the point that overlooked Clifton Bay, my telephoto lens pre-focused on the spot where the skiers could be expected to round the headland.

As the boat came swirling by, the couple criss-crossing backwards and forwards behind it, laughing, waving, and sending up huge curving plumes of white water, I held them in my sights for five long minutes, working through roll after roll with my motor drive at full stretch.

I eased the camera down from my eye with a satisfied sigh; they were good pictures. And then, sensing a movement behind me, I turned round to find myself surrounded by two very large and very black policemen who wondered, none too politely, just what I was doing, dressed as a guerrilla, hidden in the bushes,

[ 129 ]

pointing what looked like, and indeed was, a deeply offensive weapon at the island's two most famous guests.

It was a long story. At the end of it, my jaw aching from the effort of maintaining a consistently friendly grin, I was thrown into the back of a police van and driven down to the house. Jocelyn, opening his door to find me suspended for inspection, a policeman at each ankle, instantly assumed the look of a late Christmas shopper disdainfully rejecting the last scrawny turkey in the shop.

'Never seen him before in my life,' he said, and slammed the door, barely muffling a shriek of hyena-like laughter. I spent several hours in the cells, bathed in the very un-gardenia-like scent of a bunch of serious rum-drunks, wrapped in self-pity and deeply regretting the invention of photo-journalism, before the lovely Janie Stevens came to bail me out. The pictures never appeared.

When Jocelyn and I found ourselves together on the Costa Smeralda, the Aga Khan's new resort in Sardinia, I spent much of the time avoiding my proprietor, whose presence I'd begun to associate with trouble. He managed to be everywhere, none-theless, even crawling up the side of the mountain to oversee my portrait session with our host. The pictures, showing the gym-shoed spiritual-leader-turned-property-developer survey-ing his entire estate, pleased me; Jocelyn's over-casual an-nouncement as we reached the bottom of the mountain, that he seemed to have dropped the film, did not.

As I searched each inch of the mountain in the gathering twilight, I contemplated my options. Much as I appreciated the opportunities presented by my relationship with Jocelyn, neither of us expected it to last for ever. Sooner or later (and, in my current mood, probably sooner) it would be time for a change. But a change to what?

Fate, it seemed, was still on my side: there was a telegram

waiting for me at the hotel reception desk. 'MEET ME CRILLON BAR PARIS TWELVE THIRTY SEPTEMBER SIXTEENTH' it said, concluding with a one-word signature that had dizzying implications: 'VREELAND.'

Jocelyn's reaction, when I showed him the message next morning, was terse, to say the least: 'Obviously an imposter,' he said, and turned away. Although I couldn't entirely believe my luck, the telegram seemed genuine to me; it had the authentically arrogant sniff of real power about it. Hoax or not, it certainly warranted further investigation and, thanks to a last-minute lift in the Aga Khan's private jet, I arrived in the bar at the Hotel de Crillon only four minutes late for my appointment.

Four minutes too late, it seemed; of Mrs Vreeland, or, indeed, of anyone else, there was no sign. I ordered my first nervous drink and began to face up to the possibility that this was yet another of Jocelyn's complex pranks. A waiter materialised out of the darkness at the far end of the room, carrying a silver tray. The tray bore an envelope; the envelope bore my name. Inside was a stiff white sheet of *Vogue* notepaper bearing a simple, if somewhat cryptic, question. 'Who,' it asked, 'is the best dressed man in the world?'

Modesty forbore. After a few seconds' desperate cogitation, I airily scrawled a casual reply across the bottom of the page and sent it winging back into the gloom whence it came. There was a moment's pause, a rustle of black silk and out of the darkness rose the magnificently avine figure of Mrs Diana Vreeland.

She paused but a moment in passing. 'All right,' she said, 'get me some photographs,' adding, over her shoulder as she made for the door, 'Tomorrow evening will do.' I sank several stiff drinks in a state of stunned elation, called for a telephone, and went to work.

Eventually, after a great deal of confused conversation with

French telephonists who seemed to know my quarry only as 'Le Duc', I got through to his country home at Gif-sur-Yvette, just outside Paris. His wholly admirable private secretary, an expatriate American called John Utter, suggested that the easiest thing to do was simply to arrive.

The Duke, not unaccustomed to photographers, greeted me very politely, spent a few minutes speculating as to whether we were related within the meaning of the Act and, having read somewhere that I was a fellow ex-Grenadier, insisted that we practise our sword drill. As we paced up and down the heavily-manicured lawns, I watched my chances of meeting Mrs Vreeland's deadline growing slimmer and slimmer as the sun slipped further towards the horizon.

When I finally managed to get the Duke and Duchess to pose for a few last shots in the garden, desperate to raise a smile, and lacking a ladder to fall off, I put my foot through a cane garden chair instead, and guaranteed myself at least one good shot before the Duchess went off to dress for dinner.

The Duke, only slightly suspicious of my sudden interest in his wardrobe, kindly agreed to show me his impressive collection of clothes, many of which still looked up-to-date despite having been made for him just before he last saw England over thirty years previously. As his valet brought in the kilt that he tradition-ally wore to dinner, I nerved myself to ask the Duke about the way he tied what he now referred to as a necktie. Still, much to his credit, only slightly perplexed, he demonstrated beyond doubt that the thicker knot for which he was known resulted from nothing more complex that a slightly wider cut and a slightly thicker lining.

The photographs he so kindly allowed me to take, showing the Duke of Windsor tying a genuine Windsor knot, featured heavily in the twenty still slightly damp ten-by-eights that I laid on Mrs Vreeland's desk the next day. They were also, to my delight, prominent in the portfolio of my work that appeared in *Vogue*'s next issue, preceded by a short blurb that welcomed me to what was, as I was soon to discover, quite simply the greatest magazine in the world.

After a blessedly short apprenticeship snapping London socialites and London boutiques (ideally with one of each in every picture), I found myself increasingly called across the Atlantic to take briefs direct from the *Vogue* staff at their headquarters in the Graybar Building on Lexington Avenue.

At first I stayed with Willy Feilding, an artist friend of mine who lived, with his pet iguana, in a tiny flat on 62nd Street at the very top of what must have been the last building in New York without an elevator. Everything that happened during that first long, hot summer in the city seemed charged with a very special atmosphere, and even the screams of the police sirens that drifted up from the warm night-time streets through the ever-open windows seemed, somehow, symptomatic. (After a while, when I discovered that even I needed at least three hours' unpunctuated sleep, I bought Willy a small air-conditioning unit. He installed it back to front, and ran up a considerable utilities bill freshening the smog on Madison Avenue and blackening his cramped flat.)

When the contrast between the chic splendour of the late-night parties at Vreeland's tiny all-red apartment on Park Avenue and the take-outs from Chock Full O'Nuts that I shared with Feilding's smutty reptile became too much to bear, I gratefully accepted the kind offer of a guest suite in the home of a couple I'd first met in Barbados, Ronnie Tree and his American wife Marietta.

Marietta, who was a Peabody and therefore the closest America came to an indigenous aristocrat, and Ronnie, who insisted on being as British as possible and wore a brown bowler hat, had made their 79th Street home into the epitome of all that was excellent about Anglo-American relations and boasted, amongst other things, the best butler and the wickedest Martinis to be found anywhere on the East Coast.

The living symbol of this trans-Atlantic alliance was their seventeen-year-old daughter Penelope, who combined English eccentricity with American bravado in delightfully equal proportions. (Her parents had remained remarkably supportive when she'd launched her modelling career in the pages of *Vogue* wearing outfits that revealed her proportions all too well; Ronnie's nerve had broken only when he, an ex-Master of Foxhounds, came down one evening to find Penelope preparing to hit the high spots in a micro-skirt made entirely from fox brushes.)

Although New York's gossip columnists seemed determined to make us a couple, her heart and, I suspected, quite a lot else besides was given to another, a mysterious figure who rang her, anonymously, several times a day ('A Mister Michael Mouse for you, Miss Penelope,' said the butler).

Not that I had much time for night-life; I found more than enough to preoccupy me at the Graybar Building. Case-hardened by *Queen*, I fancied myself a veteran by now, perfectly accustomed to working with dominating personalities, prepared for long hours, and virtually immune to excitement. At *Vogue*, however, everything was on a grander scale; the stakes were higher, the odds on success considerably longer, and the commitment total.

The constant stream of Beautiful People that washed through the Lexington Avenue offices matched the crowds in the neighbouring Grand Central Station for noise and determination, if not punctuality. The real backbones of the magazine, as I was quick to appreciate, were the quiet professionals, none more quiet or more professional than the director of the Art Department, Alex Liberman, an impressively thin and faintly sinister figure who was also a celebrated sculptor in his own right.

Other figures on the editorial side were equally impressive: Carrie Donovan, Grace Mirabella, Robyn Butler, Pam Colin, all of whom were quick to praise, slow to condemn and generally extremely supportive of a young Englishman well out of his depth in a new and utterly bewildering environment. Mrs Vreeland's English secretary and right-hand person, Felicity Clarke, was particularly kind.

The one thing that united all these disparate figures was a responsibility to produce the biggest, the brightest and the best, an attitude that seemed to permeate the building right down to the elderly messengers. One of my earliest jobs was a children's fashion shoot, showing the infant prodigies dotted winningly around the grounds at Shugborough, and, one afternoon shortly after they'd appeared, I was touched when a greying, bespectacled figure paused on his rounds of the office to say how much he'd liked them. I thanked him and, resolving to give him a big tip at Christmas, enquired as to his name. It was Richard Avedon.

*Vogue* was, above all, a photographer's medium. The long deadlines, high-quality reproduction and constant preoccupation with style made it a deeply appealing place to work, and the long list of illustrious names under contract to the magazine included some of the greatest photographers in the business, starting with Avedon and going on to, amongst others, Peter Beard, Guy Bourdin, Henry Clarke, Bruce Davidson, Eliot Erwitt, Horst P. Horst (now concentrating on interiors), Bert Stern (a balding character who looked as if he'd stepped straight from the pages of Damon Runyon) and Gordon Parks (one of the greatest reportage men ever made).

I joined the roster at the same time as two other young photographers, Waldeck, a seriously good-looking and talented man who somehow didn't stay the course, and Arnaud de Rosnay, sportsman-photographer, who was arrested by the Russians after he'd wind-surfed across the Bering Strait and was later to disappear mysteriously and tragically on a similar crossing between Taiwan and China.

We three *ingenues* went in constant awe of most of our fellow-employees, many of whom we'd long admired from a distance and now had a chance to see in action. (One dinner with Mrs V. ended with her proposal that we 'go visit Mr Penn'. Remembering Wilton Place, I hung around in the darkness at the back of his studio, anxious to see without being seen, chain-smoking nervously until a quiet voice announced, without turning from his camera, that 'one more cigarette like that and I'll have to adjust my exposure by a sixteenth of a stop'.)

*Vogue* also had, I was proud to note, a considerable British contingent: Tony Snowdon, of course, Cecil Beaton (or Rip Van Withit, as Mick Jagger insisted on calling him) and Norman Parkinson (whom I first saw in Trinidad, at the best carnival in the world, a tall, white-haired, dancing figure towering over the frenetic crowd).

Beaton's telegraphic address was, characteristically, PINKBELL LONDON; John Cowan's was RASPUTIN and seemed equally apt. Cowan, a mad, freaky, brave and obsessively talented man, was widely rumoured to have been one of the main ingredients in Antonioni's rich stew of a film, *Blow Up*, a work which almost single-handedly retrieved the image of the professional photographer from the hands of the poodle-fakers and made all London's lensmen so difficult to live with.

Although I searched vainly for the merest inkling of myself in the film, there was no mistaking some of the component parts. Duffy, who made intransigence a way of life, was definitely in there somewhere, as was just a suspicion of Donovan (whose

[ 136 ]

impressively styled bulk I first beheld as I held a crown over Dmitri's head at his Russian Orthodox wedding).

There was also more than a tinge of McCullin here and there, not least in the scene with the down-and-outs. (Don McCullin's air of bullish gloom hides an extraordinarily sensitive intelligence; he finds life genuinely puzzling, never less so than when an excessively wrinkled lady he was photographing under Waterloo Bridge asked him for a kiss. 'Why?' he asked. 'Because you look like Captain Mark Phillips,' she replied.)

But the most easily identifiable flavour in the dish, a gamey mixture of sweet and sour, was the man I now knew to be Penelope Tree's Mister Mouse: David Bailey.

Bailey had joined *Vogue* several years earlier and his personal mythology was well documented by the time I arrived. It was said that when he first met Vreeland he had sat on her sofa staring in wild-eyed amazement as she told him, at great length and in great detail, that he was a genius. At the end of her tirade, the only sentiment he was capable of uttering was a stunned remark best translated as, 'Goodness me, Mrs Vreeland, were you but a few years younger, how I should enjoy romancing you!' (His habit of calling a spade a shovel makes him all but unquotable in polite society.)

I avoided him like the plague, affecting disdain but secretly convinced that his X-ray eye for pretension would all too quickly find me out. He, for reasons probably no more or no less comprehensible, avoided me. For several months we played a complicated game of hide-and-seek all over New York, hiding behind menus to avoid meeting in restaurants, hailing imaginary acquaintances on the street to avoid passing each other on the sidewalk, and desperately attempting to merge into coffee machines to avoid facing each other in the corridors. When we did meet, it was under somewhat unusual circumstances.

Several times a year, *Vogue* descended on Paris to cover the collections. Under the effortless direction of veteran editor Susan Train, an entire floor of the Crillon was rented and instantly transformed into a surreal cross between a strip-joint and a command-bunker as half-clad mannequins stepped warily through a maze of telephone cables to model the latest look for yet another camera.

I, easily the most junior photographer on the magazine, found myself at the far end of a very long receiving line; by the time the frocks reached me in the early hours of the morning they tended to be more than a little crumpled, as were the girls inside them. Having invested much of my youth learning lines from David Niven films, I used these occasions to polish up my seduction techniques. When I finally plucked up the courage to try out the old waiter-delivers-champagne-no-its-our-hero ploy, I did, once, manage to inveigle myself into one rather reluctant model's room. But not for long; France is, after all, the home of farce. A knock at the door, a look of alarm, and I went straight underneath the huge four-poster bed, just in time to see the model's mother's furry slippers pouncing across the carpet towards me. My attention was distracted from this awesome spectacle by a tap on the shoulder and a whispered grunt: 'Lord Lichfield, I presume?' said Bailey.

Having finally introduced ourselves, we rapidly became close friends, forming a partnership that went down particularly well with the press, who appreciated how neatly our images complemented each other. In the public prints, at least, he and I were chalk and cheese, salt and pepper, steak and onions, a simplistic view that left no room for the high regard I developed for Bailey's voracious thirst for knowledge. Back in England, he was a frequent guest at the house-parties Liz and I hosted, whenever we got the chance, at Shugborough, fully furbished in a remarkably short space of time, thanks to Liz's almost continual involvement.

A television programme that was made at the time (officially entitled 'Peer in Focus' but known to all of us as 'One Lord a Leaping') included a scene showing a 'typical' dinner-party with a guest list that included Michael Wallis, Algy Cluff, Joanna Lumley and Britt Ekland, all bravely withstanding a *Blitzkrieg* conversational assault from Bailey, whose long hair made him look like nothing so much as an aboriginal Richard III. (Dinner was announced, on the screens of the nation, by my new butler, Arthur Brearley; he and Betty are, I'm proud to say, still with me.)

As my workload increased, I found it increasingly difficult to get to Shugborough and, when I did, I deeply resented the hours I wasted travelling there. When I discovered that a motor-bike could cover the 135 miles in just under an hour and a half, I hastily dug out dim memories of a despatch riders' course I'd done in my Army days, and added a crash-helmet to my weekend wardrobe. I was encouraged in this madness by Piers Weld-Forrester, a man who once won a race from Aubrey Walk to the Dorchester by the simple expedient of travelling the entire route on the wrong side of the road; it was Piers who discovered that the network of paths that circumnavigated the ancestral home constituted an almost perfect mile of tarmacadamed track, and we promptly began a series of speed trials on Honda monkey bikes. All of this, of course, went on only after the National Trust's visitors had departed; there was no large audience to witness the women's lap record being irretrievably shattered by Princess Anne at her first attempt.

The bikes came in handy when Bradshaw and I, faced with an imminent postal strike, pooled our non-existent business talents and our names to form Rickshaw, a pirate postal service. The 1st Earl provided us with an impressive seal, Willy Feilding provided us with a stamp and we eventually shifted roughly a million letters in about six weeks.

It was a rare interlude for me; my busy schedule left me less and less time for other interests. The range of work was vast and Vreeland's passion for innovation produced commission after commission, each one exceeding the last in ambition.

Fashion stories focused more and more on the designers rather than their clothes; my first big overseas trip was to photograph Oscar de la Renta in his native Santo Domingo, a place I'd expected to be something like a cross between Trinidad and the Isle of Wight, but which proved to be far more Graham Greene than that. I also visited Cerutti, Balenciaga and even Yves St Laurent, who allowed himself to be photographed looking casual in an outfit that took literally hours to put together.

There was also quite a lot of portraiture to be done. Some pictures, like my first nude (Marsha Hunt, fresh from *Hair*) and my first *Vogue* cover (Ali McGraw, even fresher from *Love Story*) were fairly formal studio affairs.

Others were considerably looser in format, none more so than the three days I spent with Paul and Talitha Getty in their exotic home in Morocco. The *Vogue* editorial staff, who usually provided an overwhelmingly thorough background briefing, had only one thing to say on this occasion: 'Watch out for the salads.'

Regrettably, I was so busy watching out for the salads that I omitted to watch out for the caviare, the couscous and, for all I know, the bedtime cocoa; the most discreet way to describe the long, long weekend was to say that it all passed in a bit of a blur.

My occasional forays across the border into photo-journalism were a distinct contrast. I spent a fairly unenjoyable time trailing Senator McGovern's campaign trail and an enjoyable week driving round France in a Rolls-Royce, photographing, eating and talking about *haute cuisine* with Anne Scott-James, Osbert Lancaster and my latest assistant, Billy Keating, who'd now replaced Encombe, sadly missed.

I was even asked to do the odd wedding, none more odd than

that of Mick Jagger to Bianca Rosa Peréz Macias in St Tropez, an event that was at all times under constant threat from a huge and very noisy crowd made up of one part press to four parts public. The bride, an immensely elegant woman whom I'd taken out a few times in New York, asked me to give her away; the groom, an immensely likable man with whom I'd had several late-night conversations in London, failed to turn up. We waited patiently at the altar for quite a while, the organist playing louder and louder to drown the rising din of screams and yells and bangs on the locked door, before we realised that most of the noise was coming from Mick himself, desperate to be allowed into the sanctuary. He was not the neatest of bridegrooms.

As I grew used to *Vogue*'s little ways, I began to dip the odd toe into New York's highly complex social scene. It was a good time to be British in America and an increasingly wide circle of English expatriates found themselves being lionised everywhere from grand charity balls on Fifth Avenue to more Bohemian affairs in Greenwich Village. I learnt, after a while, to recognise the hard-core Beautiful People who seemed to turn up everywhere, many of them associated in one way or another with *Vogue*: Baby Jane Holzer, Kenneth J. Lane, Ahmad and Mica Ertegun, Chessy Rayner, and, everywhere you looked, Andy Warhol.

I was privileged one evening to be amongst the audience for one of Warhol's celebrated happenings, a deeply mysterious and apparently meaningless series of non-events that climaxed, somewhat prematurely, when a man wrapped from head to foot in bandages tripped over a loose end and made a percussive descent into the orchestra pit. I was also privileged to hear hundreds of his little epigrams, gnomic statements that always sounded terrific the moment he said them, always seemed incredibly vacuous in the cold light of morning and always stuck in the mind, for weeks afterwards, like burrs.

His most famous remark, to the effect that sooner or later everybody would be famous for all of fifteen minutes, struck an increasingly resonant chord. Slowly but surely, my name began to appear in the gossip columns: 'Lord Lichfield, blue-blooded photographer, decorative member of the international set and very fancy dresser. . .', ran one accolade. I wasn't at all sure that I cared for 'decorative' but the reference to my clothes was all too typical. New York seemed to be fascinated by my wardrobe and when I remarked, rather acidly, that everybody else in the city seemed still to be dressing from the pages of the Brooks Brothers catalogue, there were small headlines everywhere. I was even challenged to do a tour of the trendier boutiques in town with a fashion journalist and photographer in tow. (My sponsors were more than a little piqued that the only purchases I made were at the wonderful Army-Navy Store.)

When I found myself appearing on Eleanor Lambert's Best Dressed List for the third year in succession, I did pause briefly to wonder what the family would have made of it; I comforted myself with the knowledge that the Admiral had impressed the Chinese at Canton by sending his emissaries ashore dressed in the splendid but thoroughly irrelevant uniforms of Thames watermen.

It was head-turning stuff. The height of my fifteen-minutes'-worth was probably the days I spent being sculpted by Adèle Rootstein, who'd decided that my particular profile was just what she needed for a new range of store window dummies, the story ended sadly many years later when I found models of myself in a tatty Carnaby Street window, painted black and bedizened with Afro wigs.

One firm of clothes wholesalers was impressed enough by this nonsense to offer me the chance of designing my own clothes, which were subsequently marketed under an allusively aristocratic brand name (we rejected Lord Luvverduck as being, how should one say, just a little prosaic). The promotional tour I'd promised in support of the venture coincided with my much-publicised relationship with Britt Ekland (further highly fictional details of which may be found by the curious in the pages of her autobiography).

On the first leg of our trip, Britt found herself the only woman in a huge Dallas convention hall, a potentially traumatic event to which she adjusted remarkably quickly; I had considerably more difficulty coming to terms with the fact that my designs appeared to have been 'interpreted' in an uncommonly fluid fashion which made the resulting garments look like nothing on earth.

Their tailors may well have been terrible but their lawyers were nonpareils; I found myself tied to the remainder of the promotional tour without any influence over the clothes I was supposed to be promoting. Gamely I soldiered on, dressing myself in my own clothes from Tommy Nutter, Blades and Burlington Bertie, stubbornly changing the subject whenever it turned to fashion and eventually arriving in Los Angeles where I treated myself to a bungalow in what was then probably the best hostelry on the West Coast, the Beverly Hills Hotel.

Exhausted from morning after morning of breakfast television interviews, I stripped and stretched out on the bed, utterly fascinated by the ornate chandelier that hung above me. (A chandelier in a bungalow? Only in America. . . .)

The first time the chandelier shivered I put it down to a trick of the light. The second time, I remembered everything I'd heard about earthquakes and threw myself out of the window. As I lay there, wearing only a watch, clinging on to the grass for support, I heard footsteps behind me and, having no really simple explanation in mind, grinned widely at the three dinner-jacketed businessmen as they walked past me. They looked at me as if I was entirely mad. There must, I thought, be better ways of making a living.

# [ 10 ]

It was faintly humiliating to find, on my flying visits to Aubrey Walk, that Lichfield Studios seemed to be managing quite happily without me; at times I found myself standing, useless amidst the purposeful bustle, wondering if perhaps I wasn't becoming surplus to requirements. The developing, printing and distributing of the stream of images I was now manufacturing with ever-growing facility, and the provision of the support services on which I was fast becoming totally dependent (arranging itineraries, cleaning kit, auditioning models, and parrying mackintosh) meant that I now needed at least two full-time assistants and a highly capable secretary. I was lucky enough to be well provisioned with both.

When my first secretary, Liz Ramsay, left to get married, I was delighted to be able to procure the services of Mary Burr for a while, before she was succeeded by Jennifer Marshall, admirably pre-tempered for the shot-and-shell atmosphere in which we worked by previous long service in a large London advertising agency. Jennifer's place was taken, in turn, by Felicity McDonald, an incredibly capable woman who, having already survived the rigours of working for two other busy photographers (Barry 'Crossed Sellotape' Lategan and my new brother-in-law Geoffrey Shakerley), at least knew what to expect. I have been privileged to watch the aptly-named Felicity developing, over the years, an almost Zen-like calm whose tireless, patient strength underpins the operation to this day.

Johnny Encombe's place as an assistant was taken by Billy

Keating, an upwardly mobile young man who was followed, in due course, by Nicole le Vien, a wonderfully mercurial figure who died, tragically, from meningitis in the late Seventies.

Sara Heaton, another assistant, had a rather 'county' façade that tended to collapse completely at irregular intervals, never more constructively than when she turned cartwheels on the sacred turf at Newmarket to produce one of the rare documented examples of a genuine smile from Lester Piggott. Her successor, Richard Dawkins, whose outward aspect of young yeoman farmer was belied by his extraordinary delicacy of touch in the darkroom (and elsewhere, I'm told), joined me from John Cowan and left me for Bailey, from whom I was lucky enough to be able to borrow him in times of need.

Each and every one of these excellent people willingly suffered what must have been constant frustration and frequent pain, working with a nervy and unreasonably demanding autocrat all too liable to sudden ego attacks in which he succumbed to the ultimate delusion of believing his own press-cuttings. I found to my amazement that, despite the appalling conditions, my work-force steadily grew larger and stayed longer; grateful for all the help I could get, I thanked heaven for them all, and tried not to begrudge the regular salary rises their continuing presence seemed, so tacitly, to demand.

The speed of my inevitable mutation into a corporate body quickened with every job we successfully completed; anxious not to have all its eggs in one camera-bag, the Lichfield Corporation began to make a few tentative moves towards diversifying its interests. Annacat had, as the Sixties wound down, sickened and then passed away, quite painlessly; twice bitten and determined not to be caught out again, I shied away from further involvement with either men's or women's clothing and dabbled instead in another consuming passion: food.

When I (quite literally) bumped into one of London's trendiest tailors at a New York party, the conversation between us turned, with what seemed like majestic inevitability, to restaurants and restauranting; a few months later, with the backing of forty of his liveliest clients, most of them actors, Doug Hayward and I opened Burkes in Bond Street, as English an establishment as anyone could hope for, given a Swiss chef, a Scottish designer and Italian waiters. It was a great place to eat, particularly if you were a proprietor, but it never made much money.

My biggest gamble by far was my interest in a less than conventional musical that I'd seen in New York and which I felt sure would be the biggest thing to hit England since *Lilac Time.* *Hair,* when it opened in London, did very nicely, thank you, and the proceeds of this brief flirtation with show business paid for the fulfilment of another secret dream, a small and completely overgrown plot of earth on a tiny and extremely beautiful West Indian island.

Mustique was virtually invented by Colin Tennant, single-handedly, a man straight from the pages of Conrad who had style, ambition and financial acuity in almost equal measure; when he parted with a ten-acre slice of his deserted fiefdom as a wedding present for Princess Margaret, the island slowly started to become a popular home-from-home for people who appreciated its absence of most modern amenities such as hairdressing salons, souvenir shops and press photographers.

Building anything larger than a coal-shed on my jungle patch was patently beyond my means, at least for the present; the few guilty hours that I snatched there whenever I could (camping out, for the moment, in a gatehouse I had built for myself in Princess Margaret's grounds) were persistently overshadowed by the nagging awareness that I ought to be elsewhere, earning at least the price of a bucket of mortar and a handful of limestone bricks.

Aubrey Walk, Mustique and Shugborough were the three

fixed points in my fluid compass; none of them saw me for more than a week at a time. Even Shugborough, its peace now recovered from the roar of motorbikes, exercised an ambivalent tug on my heart-strings; the purse-strings were still, perforce, fairly tight.

I almost pined for the early days. Life seemed a lot easier when every little ten-bob note pressed into my hand had represented one small step towards another lens, another box of paper, another evening out. Everything was much more abstract now; all I knew was that I simply had to keep working.

When, on one of my last trips for *Vogue*, I was sent to photograph Aristotle Onassis' enormous yacht, the *Christina*, its lavishly appointed interior turned out to contain many features better suited, in my opinion, to Maidenhead rather than the Mediterranean. (I was particularly puzzled by the swimming-pool that converted into a dance-floor at the push of a button; since the *Christina* had more than enough space to accommodate several Municipal Baths and at least two Lyceum Ballrooms, the point of the exercise rather escaped me.) When the millionaire yachtsman came aboard and found me in his dining saloon, deeply involved in the study of a massive, early eighteenth-century wine-cooler by Paul de Lamerie, I assuaged his all-too-visible suspicion that I was about to slip it into my pocket by rolling up my sleeve to reveal, yet again, Drummond's bounty. The tattooed seahorse matched exactly the emblem chased into the side of the silver bucket; the wine-cooler was one of the pieces we'd lost in the Shugborough sale. When I offered to buy it back from him (if and when my boat came in), the look of total incredulity that dawned over his none-too-chiselled features was answer enough; if I aspired to repurchasing family heirlooms, I had a great deal of earning still to do, and not necessarily with *Vogue*.

'John Thomas' had managed to sell a few shots to Ernestine

Carter at the *Sunday Times* before somebody queried the dubious pseudonym; Mrs Vreeland did not take kindly to 'her' photographers selling their work elsewhere. She, and her glossy contract, had proved literally enchanting, dangerously so; perhaps it was time to break free of the lotus-eating sunlit uplands by Grand Central Station and up the ante yet again. I began to investigate the only alternative source of honest work I knew: British magazines.

Rather than crawl back to *Queen* (which, in Jocelyn's increasing absence, was temporarily slackening anyway) and all too prepared to pay a degrading price for my greedy arrogance in seeking to better myself yet further, I signed up promptly with what I remembered as being the dullest periodical around: *The Radio Times*. I should have learnt, by now, that people will insist on changing things when one's back is turned; whilst I'd been away they'd installed full colour, bright copy and quality graphics, making the magazine, then and now, a valuable source of work for professional portraitists.

*Queen*'s place was taken, after a while and in a very minor way, by *Ritz*, a useful little outlet run jointly by Davids Bailey and Litchfield (little or no relation); they paid peanuts but they had good taste. English *Vogue* also commissioned occasional snaps from me but, even under the stern control of Beatrix Miller, it sometimes had to run very hard indeed to keep up with its more ambitious American cousin.

A garbled telephone call from a publication that announced itself simply as 'The Enquirer' heralded the beginning of the glossiest job I had for quite a while: would I care to go to Hollywood to take pictures of ten super-stars? Having long admired the respectable editorial stance of the *Philadelphia Enquirer*, I eagerly agreed and found myself working with a curious figure called Henry Gris, a Latvian journalist with one withered arm. Despite his repeated assurances that all would be well, the doors of the famous remained stubbornly unopen and it was only when we introduced ourselves to an ex-wife of Dean Martin, Jeanne, that things really started to work.

Jeanne, a delightfully pretty woman, pointed us straight to her one-time spouse, who welcomed us to what seemed to be an almost entirely empty house; his fixtures and fittings were apparently marooned in some endless custody wrangle. But, since he still had a few of his platinum records left on the wall, I persevered with the idea I'd worked out and asked him to pose with a treasured possession. The request propelled him straight to the bar where he upended a bottle of gin into a cocktail shaker, added ice, and whispered 'Vermouth' over the surface. 'Sometimes,' he confided, 'I just point the bottle in the direction of Italy.'

Raquel Welch was unable, at first, to see me 'because she's had a landslide', an intriguing thought, but Glenn Ford, James Coburn, Rhonda Fleming and Angie Dickinson (whose legs I had long admired from afar) all made me welcome and, in many cases, introduced me to their spouses. As the doorman of the Beverly Hills Hotel ushered me into the cab that was to take me to my penultimate appointment, he whispered I should be sure and talk to my prospective sitter's wife. The senior serviceperson who greeted me and explained that my host wasn't ready yet merely chuckled when I asked if I could talk to Mrs Rock Hudson: it was he.

Natalie Wood and Robert Wagner, the last pair of names on my list, proved totally charming and both enquired, casually, as to the identity of the journalist with whom I was working. The name of the eminent Gris sent visible shudders down both of their spines. My employer, it seemed, was not the *Philadelphia Enquirer* but the *National Enquirer*, a supermarket-counter tabloid whose staple fare was a piquant combination of *paparazzi* photos, steamy gossip and three-inch three-word headlines ('Pig

Eats Boy' on the issue I finally found). Blushing furiously, I made my excuses and left as soon as I decently could.

The photographs, deeply decorous by the paper's usual standards, appeared as promised and indeed earnt me a handsome fee; it felt like a narrow squeak nonetheless. Thinking it wise to spread my interests yet wider, I finally volunteered for commerce.

The British advertising industry, never one to leave a bandwagon unambushed for long, was beginning to recognise photography's new status by offering some impressively gainful employment to a handful of the country's better-known professionals. (Better-known, rather than simply better, of course; they were, in their own words, selling the sizzle not the steak.) Perhaps still not untainted by a faint tinge of ancestral pride where 'trade' was concerned or, much more likely, simply all too aware from my days with Wallis that agencies could be hard task-masters, I hadn't exactly rushed to introduce myself to this rising young market; now, needs musting, I appointed my first commercial agent, a florid and utterly unlikely figure called Jeremy Banks who, true to his word that he knew everyone worth knowing, returned a few days later bearing a rich, ripe, peach of a job.

The client was Bayer Pharmaceutical, the brief a series of pictures for an up-market corporate campaign and the theme was Shakespeare's 'Seven Ages of Man'. The photographs were to be black and white, which was good, the company's products seemed to be entirely ethical, which was better, and they were offering, best of all, a hitherto almost unheard of amount of money. It all sounded deeply suspicious.

Illustrating the Bard's famous gallery of archetypes (the Infant, mewling and puking, the Schoolboy, creeping like snail, the Soldier, quick in quarrel, and so forth) proved, in fact, to be an extremely interesting commission. Unlike my previous portrait work, the images we were after had to ignore, rather than emphasise, the character of the models we used, cutting through all the individual whims and quirks to reach something much more universal. The challenge was, in a curious way, not (as before) to put character into the pictures but to drain it out.

The shoot, which took me far longer than it ought to have done, was fascinating; one particular shot (of a be-spectacled, be-denimed figure, crouched over his books and bearded, indubitably, like the pard) commemorates one of the best things to happen to me in what was already a very good year: the arrival of Peter Kain. Pedro, as he rapidly became known, has more right than most to treat the meagre title of 'assistant' with the disdain that, in his case, it deserves; fifteen years' incredibly loyal service, laughing like a drain at my jokes for the fortieth time as he quietly puts the camera the right way up in my hand deserves something far better than that; Jilly Cooper came close to it when she said he 'looks like the disciple whom Jesus loved'.

Before the Bayer job began, I'd assumed that the largeish sums of lucre involved would be a salve or, failing that, an elastic bandage for my wounded pride: I fully expected to be demoted to the role of mere illustrator, supplying Identikit pictures on demand to satisfy the callow whims of some adolescent art-director. Nothing could have been further from the truth; apart from anything else, I certainly felt I'd earnt every penny of my fee.

Many of the clients for whom I now began to work seemed only too happy to accept my own ideas as to how we might present their often old products in new guises and I relished the problems thrown up by these exercises in the engineering of images. (Problem: how to show a series of television sets with, to my eye, rather nasty reproduction antique consoles? Answer: take the insides out and use them to frame a set of famous

[ 151 ]

landmarks, an approach which earnt us a fresh set of funny looks at Customs.)

Some companies actively demanded innovation; Daimler, for instance, commissioned several photographers to re-invent the image of their cars. The first picture I took (showing headlights beaming out into the dawn from the lavishly lit interior of Blenheim Palace) was a merely technical triumph; the second, with the car halted on the surface of a lake by a traffic policeman in an aqualung outfit, pleased me much more (the original idea, drawn from the worst of those ah-lovely snaps in which *Picture Post* specialised, had been meant to include the reason for the hold-up: Caution, plastic ducks crossing).

I was beginning, by now, to appreciate the difference between the way editorial and advertising pictures worked. Readers of the glossy magazines in which my work appeared usually headed straight past the ads *en route* for the main attraction: the editorial pages for which they'd paid their money in the first place. My job was to buttonhole them, as politely as possible, as they passed. It was all, as my grandmother might have said, a Matter of Tone; one had to neither mutter nor scream, but insist nonetheless.

Once buttonholed, the reluctant passer-by rarely had the time or the inclination to linger; the shot had to communicate as concisely and effectively as possible, whilst still leaving a memorable and attractive impression. What that impression was, or, rather, what it ought to be was, to a certain extent, up to me. Somehow, I couldn't help thinking about Inner Essences.

I found some products much easier to deal with than others. As with the 'celebrities' of my earlier years, the easiest were the ones which had been around long enough to have instituted for themselves a fairly clear network of emotional association with which one could work. If the product was something I actually used myself, the process of exploration became even more exciting, never more so than with a certain celebrated raincoat. The Burberry (never, please, a 'mac') has a small but solidly established place in the mythology of the English countryside; to some people it's even more evocative than a pair of green wellies, and the more worn the better; ten years after he died, I found my grandfather's still hanging in the gun-room and it fitted me perfectly.

Working with Jean Shrimpton had taught me that the best fashion shoots are the ones where the models look as if they own the clothes, so the proposition put to me by Burberry's Peter Matthews and Art Director Chris Hudson over lunch at the Trattoo seemed to make a lot of sense. When they offered me a chance to both have my cake and eat it, by photographing myself myself, I all too eagerly agreed.

Capturing my own image in this way ('Self-Portrait by Patrick Lichfield') proved, predictably I suppose, far from easy. The problem was not how to pose, or smile, or even look comfortable (I hadn't spent years issuing instructions to others without picking up at least a few tricks of the trade), nor was it anything to do with draining away my personality (what there was of it they'd either have to like or lump); I just never knew when the self-timer would go off.

After we'd wasted several rolls of film capturing either a fuzzy blur of badly timed arrival or a frozen rictus of anticipation, we rewrote the brief slightly, made quite sure there was nobody else in the frame and retitled the pictures 'Lord Lichfield Photographed by Himself'. (Richard Dawkins, standing in for a temporarily hospitalised Pedro, was the hitherto unacknowledged ghost in the machine.)

The Burberry was, and is, in its own unique way, an English institution. So, indisputably, was my favourite portrait sitter from this period, Lord Stockton, then Mr Harold Macmillan, a man to whom I'd been first introduced only minutes after I'd driven into his gatepost. (Locked in the darkroom all the previous night, and anxious to make a good impression, I'd asked Michael for a nerve-tonic.)

When I returned to Birch Grove House some fifteen years later, to photograph him on his eighty-fifth birthday, I found the senior statesman emanating an impressive, if rather gloomy, air of determined *gravitas*. Utterly impassive, he sat through my entire repertoire of cheerful chatter without batting an eyelid. Silenced at last, I eventually ended up simply tripping the shutter virtually at random, convinced I would never get anything other than a long series of identical portraits of a man who looked as if he had just noticed an unpleasant aroma.

'Not going too well, is it?' he grunted after a while.

'Well, no, sir, as a matter of fact it's terrible. . . .'

'Serves you right, you know,' he said. 'Gatepost. Sixty-six. Haven't forgotten,' and unfroze immediately into the superbly consummate character actor that, at heart, he is. It was one of the nicest shoots I've ever done.

When Kodak, itself something of an institution, commissioned me to produce a calendar based on a slice of my own past, I was slightly disturbed to find that the images of Harrow that I had been carrying around inside my head since boyhood now bore little or no resemblance to reality. What had originally been intended as a series of reportage shots became something much more interesting; the re-creation of a dream. As we set about 'interpreting' the place, mixing genuine schoolboys and hired models with liberal abandon, I tried to remember what Warhol had said about a fake being more real than the original; I couldn't quite grasp it but the pictures worked well all the same.

I also worked for the Army, doing some television commercials with a production company I set up with Dugald Rankin; they were something of a contrast to the short film we made about a tramp called Spider who lived out of a pram in which he kept a wind-up gramophone (which worked) and a telephone (which didn't). Spider's highly mythologised version of himself was made with our own money and the scale proved a salutary contrast to some of the more lunatic antics of the expense-no-object admen. On one shoot, a packaging shot for a fabric softener, the brief decreed dandelion clocks, in November. Rather than miss the deadline, the agency insisted on running up so many not-quite-perfect working models of the unseasonable weed it would have been cheaper to fly everybody off to the Antipodes for a week or two instead. I kept mum; I'd had enough of abroad for the time being.

The longer I stayed in England, the more I learnt about its landscape, a rich and varied theme that began to loom larger in my work. Nonetheless, when British American Tobacco commissioned me to do a series of portraits of England, I baulked a little at the scale of the task. (As an inveterate smoker, promoting cigarettes worried me not at all at the time; the whole topic was considerably less contentious then and I'd already taken portraits of Jeanne Moreau, Kurt Jurgens and Tony Perkins for Winston.) The thing that really worried me was the prospect of having to condense the whole vast nebulous assortment of dimly perceived associations that meant England to me into a dozen or so frozen moments. What was 'England' to me, after all?

I knew what it was not; it wasn't, for instance, the Disneyland fantasy I'd attended on behalf of a travel company client, where wenches poured synthetic mead over the court jester's poly-styrene cap and bells. And it wasn't the country house idyll Hugh Hefner so patently had in mind when he offered me 'a Pimm' and a game of 'Cro-kaay' (played in long grass with the side of the mallet).

*Vogue* in general, with its blatant Anglophilia, and Mrs Vree-land in particular, with her talent for spotting a strong idea, had a lot to answer for in all this; one of the briefing cables I received read, simply: 'Henley Regatta is from July 10 to 13 and we would adore you to photograph prettiest girls in London with niftiest chaps under parasols and dripping willows in boats Vreeland.' (Mrs Vreeland had a justly famous reputation for the exuberant brio of her briefs:

'Bailey,' she said once, 'fetch me the pink of India!' When, deeply puzzled and having finally resorted to photographing the sub-continent through a rose-coloured filter, he put the pictures on her desk, she looked distinctly crestfallen.

'But Bailey, the pink of India is blue.')

John McHugh and Trumbull Barton, whose remarkably hospitable New York brownstone was the closest thing to home I ever saw on the North American continent, were very much in a minority; everybody else in America knew just what England looked like; they'd seen it in the glossy magazines (and, it must be said, in quite a few of my photographs). In a vain attempt to prove that there was more to little-old-Swinging-England than dolly-birds living in sin with swan-uppers on the top floor of immaculately thatched tower blocks, I invited a party of *Vogue* staffers across the pond for a little light shooting. The weekend was a total disaster. Jerry Zipkin, latterly employed as Nancy Reagan's 'walker' (whatever that might be), arrived with nine suitcases that were still being unpacked when it was time to leave three days later; one editor wore a pink fun-fur coat that frightened most of the feathered population of the area into the next county, together with quite a few of the local worthies; and Shugborough's wiring, never healthy at the best of times and now overloaded by innumerable electric fires, eventually collapsed completely under the additinal burden of a male guest's plug-in curlers.

When I discovered that the B.A.T. job was to photograph English towns rather than countrysides, I wasn't sure whether to be relieved or not but, as so often before, all of my Inner Essence problems vanished in the face of the sheer delight and the sheer difficulty of the job in hand, finding one really good picture in each town. In Aberdeen we photographed the fishing fleet, in Oxford the dons, in Northampton we photographed a pork pie factory and in Sunderland I became one of the few hereditary peers to be a member of a working-men's club. And, true to the institutional stereotype, it rained: in Portsmouth, in Southampton, in Coventry, in Sheffield and, worst of all, in London.

On the last day before the deadline we sat in Trader Vic's drinking *mai-tais* in a vain attempt to conjure up a little tropical colour; half an hour later, leaning perilously out over the high parapet of a neighbouring hotel in a sudden burst of late sunshine, I caught three of the most successful images I've ever taken. Instinct will out, particularly in times of stress.

As with the Bayer job, one of the pictures we used includes a model assistant, John White. Chalky, as he is predictably known, is a dedicated black and white photographer, always a good sign, and he looks not unlike an apprentice pirate; his street-smart attitude is the perfect complement to Pedro's quieter virtues, and his arrival marked the final conglomeration of a finer support team than any photographer deserves.

Both of them have, over the years, accompanied me all over the world, most notably into the Southern Hemisphere where fate, having noticed my growing attachment to England, decided to despatch me forthwith. A clothing company that made perfectly good, if rather boring, frocks sent us on a fashion shoot that began in Amsterdam, moved on to New York and San Francisco, then took in Fiji, stayed for a while in Sydney and finally terminated, somewhat the worse for wear, in Papua New Guinea where I asked a tribesman to pose with his most treasured possession and he chose a small piglet; very tasty it

[ 157 ]

was too. On a later trip we photographed wedding dresses in the deserts of Mexico and jungles of Brazil; it all seemed to make perfect sense at the time.

The Far East, where we were later to photograph twenty cities for Cathay Pacific, enchanted me, especially Australia, where I admired the fact that the population seemed to divide clearly into two mutually opposing camps, the very British and the very not.

In Sydney's rather grand Wentworth Hotel one morning, anxious to see how my previous evening's speech had gone down, I tiptoed out into the early-morning corridor, intent on purloining a neighbour's newspaper, only to find myself, stark naked, locked out of my room. The total *sang froid* with which the receptionist greeted my appearance at his desk, inelegantly swaddled in the *Sydney Morning Herald*, was impressive to behold. Very British, I thought, as were, predictably, the four very cool ladies I was asked to photograph as epitomes of Australasian beauty; I'm afraid I over-reacted slightly and threw in a wild card of my own, a far less self-possessed study of my own choice, flagrantly naked on a rather health-and-efficiency rock, on Bondi Beach.

The very nots, in contrast, believed in 'hairv'n fun', an innocuous enough description that covers a multitude of lurid sins that range from the totally unmentionable to the barely credible, as with the air hostess who boarded one flight having ingested something that drove her to attempt a world-record-breaking bid to seduce every male passenger under the age of sixty in as short a time as possible. (Fully prepared to lie back and think of England, I was a little disappointed when a bucket of iced water and a pair of handcuffs did for her before she reached me.)

There was a time when all this would have struck me as ever such a jolly wheeze; now I found myself increasingly grateful to get back to the respectable peace and quiet of Shugborough where I was, at last, beginning to take an active role in the running of the estate.

After considerable thought, I began by talking to (rather than at) the trustees and found, to my delight, that some of them could be persuaded to retire in favour of my own nominees.

The family solicitor, Bobby Lyons, was replaced by the somewhat more ebullient figure of Quentin Crewe, gourmet writer, *bon viveur* and landowner in his own right. (Despite his cruel confinement to a wheelchair, Quentin was also a keen traveller; when he moved to France a few years later his place was taken by a respected captain of industry, Lord Nelson of Stafford.)

Patrick Winnington, a much loved uncle (and husband of a much loved aunt), was the only one of the initial trio with whom I had ever felt any rapport; he stayed, for the moment, to be replaced eventually by another relation, also a relatively successful landowner: the Duke of Westminster.

The third trusteeship, originally held by Edward Morley-Fletcher, was thrust upon the man who, above all others, had re-opened my eyes to the full glory of the British countryside and sowed in me the first small seeds of a passion for the cultivation, preservation and general veneration of trees; a man who is, as his name perhaps suggests, both wild and wise in equal measure. The Thane of Cawdor (for it is he) is also, amongst manifold other honorifics, the Wittiest Letter-Writer in the kingdom; bound volumes of his epistolary ingenuity are kept close by the medicine cabinet at all times.

This second, and rather more mobile, generation of trustees had the advantage that we could all meet for discussions on-site rather than in boardrooms in remote City offices; the move towards a more active, more involved policy of estate-management was completed when we took the day-to-day stewardship of the property away from an efficient, if somewhat cold-blooded, firm of land-agents and entrusted it to one man, a local worthy with an astonishingly high reputation for efficiency whose biggest burden in life is to be the butt of constant cleverness about his name: Major Haszard (an appellation that does scant justice to his astuteness, intelligence and coolness under fire.)

The confidence I drew from these sturdy supporters encouraged me to take active steps towards establishing a proper dialogue with my co-tenants, the National Trust and the local County Council. The three-cornered relationship we have (more or less) successfully maintained has not been without its more ironic moments: I have to admit the childish glee I derived from once informing the curators of the house that my expert guest who had so cleverly spotted their error in dating of the remaining Paul de Lamerie silverware was the drummer with the Rolling Stones, a Mr Charles Watts.

This reactivation of my interest in the Shugborough estate meant, of course, that even when there I was rarely able to relax, an activity which, since I somehow felt I'd never really mastered it, I resolved not to regret. When a magazine sent us off to do a where-are-they-now series on great models of the past, I found most of my erstwhile colleagues in East Grinstead, living comfortable lives as the comfortable wives of prosperous stock-brokers.

For my part, I sought out more and more work (and a bit more play), doing my best not to notice the fact that I was developing a habit of frequently falling into a sleep so deep that nothing, save a policeman crashing through my bedroom window, could rouse me. Sensing that this increasingly frequent disability was symptomatic of some fundamental failure, I guiltily ignored it for a year or more until, after one airport-bound taxi-ride too many had ended back at Aubrey Walk with the meter still running, I consulted a specialist; he diagnosed narcolepsy, said Lenny Bruce had it too and told me there was nothing to be done; whereupon it disappeared immediately and has yet, touch wood, to be seen or heard of again.

The continuous burning of my candle at both ends created a thickening pall of smoke, much of which seemed to hang persistently over the gossip columns where my faintly-tarnished reputation skulked uneasily like Frankenstein's monster. As I pointed out, time after time, to those few society diarists with whom I remained on speaking terms, despite my refusal to draw a divide between business and pleasure, the nature of my relationship with the undeniably beautiful women in whose company I was lucky to be seen was rarely less than professional. They nodded sagely, crossed out the words 'Ladies' Man' from their copy, and inserted 'Professional Ladies' Man' in its place.

Grinning as widely as possible under the circumstances, I attempted, yet again, to persuade myself that no publicity was bad publicity and made the most of it. The perilously unsteady pedestal on which I'd been placed, clearly labelled Expert on Beauty, had at the least the small virtue of bringing in work from the women's magazines.

I photographed Barbara Christie Miller twice, once in a tiara and ballgown, and once in a Barbour in the rain; she looked equally beautiful in both. I photographed Angela Rippon in profile, literally showing a side of her with which few were familiar. I photographed Susan George, Olivia Newton John, Diana Rigg, the Duchess of Bedford, Stephanie Beecham, Gayle Hunnicutt, and, striking a blow for the less than famous, a lovely traffic wardeness whose wilful way with her uniform may have been influenced by the fact that it was her last day in the job. I photographed Ava Gardner (who would have been Cousin Ava if her relationship with my eccentric cousin had ever borne fruit) and I photographed Faye Dunaway, on a day trip to New York, by Concorde from London, in four minutes flat. I photographed the most beautiful women in Hollywood for diamond merchant Harry Winston and I photographed the most beautiful little girls in England for Pears Soap. When I was asked to compere Miss World it seemed like a natural progression.

My co-host was Sacha Distel and he and I at one stage of the proceedings were despatched to our dressing-room deep in the bowels of the Albert Hall with strict instructions on no account to change anything about our appearance lest we interfere with continuity. We managed to open a bottle of champagne nonetheless, and settled ourselves in for a short but thoroughly locker-room chat about the merits and demerits of the most beautiful women in the world whilst the television audience was treated to a short film showing the international contestants going about their ordinary daily lives, riding horses, baking apple pies and helping little old gentlemen across the road. (M. Distel was, I think, much pre-occupied with Miss Australia's 'berm'.)

We both, after a while, noticed a distantly booming echo, growing louder and closer, and clarifying rapidly into the sound of running footsteps echoing through the vast empty spaces that separated us from the BBC Outside Broadcast vans, busily broadcasting outside. The door burst open and two technicians threw themselves at our throats. Our radio mikes, it seemed, were still live.

I followed this episode with one yet more disgraceful still when I was invited to photograph the Miss Universe contest in Manila. As the personal guest of President and Madame Marcos, no expense was spared; my suite was fitted out with everything I could possibly desire: a monogrammed dressing-gown, a pair of monogrammed pyjamas and two of the most beautiful maids I have ever seen in my life (unmonogrammed as far as I could tell).

Madame Marcos, an extraordinary woman not known as the Iron Butterfly for nothing, was heavily into her Green Revolution at the time, and I agreed to take pictures of a lavish mock-Nobel prize-giving ceremony at which large medals were awarded to whichever of the world's great and good could be persuaded to fly to the Philippines to collect them.

When a famous Moscow physicist failed to show, I was pressed into service in his place; as I stood there in my red sash, trying not to drop my gong and wishing I could remember the Russian for quark, I wondered what my grandfather would have made of such a deeply spurious occasion and swiftly decided to think about something else instead.

This mad and distinctly hectic progress (which included a long lost weekend, sharing a room with Bailey in Mexico, playing maiden-aunts-and-milk-bottles with magnums of champagne) came to a dizzying halt when I awoke one morning to find myself in Japan, at the end of a very sticky affair with the widow of a deposed dictator, feeling utterly exhausted and deeply homesick.

I rang my sister in England and begged, pleaded, insisted that she organise a house-party for the coming weekend, a welcome home present that was to include, please, as many fresh, clean, beautiful, intelligent, and utterly charming English-rose-types as she could possibly find at such short notice. Shugborough has never looked lovelier; I was in love within the hour and engaged within the year to Lady Leonora Grosvenor, sister of the Duke of Westminster.

My wife took on what I can now see must have been an awesome challenge, allying herself to a deep-dyed workaholic with a playboy image who was showing every sign of allowing himself to be turned into a small, but distinctly public, institution. Our life together started high-profile and went straight on up.

The burglars who broke into Aubrey Walk one night, the latest in a long line of thieves, were patently amateur; although they took care to go through every picture on file, they (rather endearingly I thought) took only the contact sheets, leaving the far more precious negatives behind. They also, less endearingly, took all my cameras.

We replaced the Hasselblads immediately but I hesitated over the decision as to what to do about the 35 mm. These smaller, less studio-oriented cameras were showing a developing tendency to accrete into systems, diversifying from a single body and a single lens into a fascinating array of spare bodies, extra lenses, motor-drives, flash units and who-knows-what-next; a decision to opt for one particular manufacturer's system would, given the expense of all that gear, imply a commitment that lasted, if not till death, then at least for a very long while. It was at just that moment that my excellent new agent, David Lynch, came up with a suggestion from Olympus; was I open to some kind of reciprocal deal? Rarely one to look a gift-horse in the gums, I made an exception in this case; since they would presumably be looking for a degree of public endorsement from me, it was to a certain extent, a matter of honour that I should be genuinely happy with the machinery. Not only that, of course, but the quality of the cameras would, all too obviously, be reflected in the quality of the pictures I took with them, pictures on which my livelihood depended. I made some extensive enquiries.

The new range from Olympus weren't Leicas, but then again only Leicas were. The OM range was, on the other hand, not only as good as anything I'd used before but also considerably lighter, a major consideration given the distances they'd have to be carried. My signature on the contract with Olympus marked yet another small step on my transformation, a journey I happily took alongside Donovan, McCullin, Fincher and, of course, the ubiquitous Bailey.

The first television commercial, in which the lovable cockney cameraman is discovered assisting the photographic endeavours of a pair of innocent tourists, was supposedly set outside Buckingham Palace, but actually filmed at Greenwich, complete with a sentry-box and a no expense spared sentry to go in it. When I insisted that the actor they'd hired to impersonate the average guardsman looked distinctly cherubic, my own rather more ravaged features were pressed into service. And so my insidious climb towards invidious fame continued, laying my wife and myself open to the attentions of a whole new sub-category of the Great British Public, the ones who care not a whit for either gossip columns or photographic magazines but never forget a face. ('It's you, isn't it! Look, love, it's him!')

I also began to crop up, with what must have been irritating monotony, on television and radio shows, including mid-market quiz games like *Call My Bluff* and *Desert Island Discs* (but not, as yet, *This Is Your Life*; Leonora, quite rightly, drew the line at having to smile sweetly at long-lost relations from Australia). When I was asked to pose for Madame Tussaud's, I almost told them that, if they searched the basements of Soho, a few tinted mannequins might yet remain to be found, then thought better of it and settled for trying to look as much like my image as possible. (Unveiling my own waxwork was a very odd feeling, surpassed for strangeness only by the model of me that stands in the Bradford Museum of Photography, which not only moves but talks as well.)

These jack-in-the-box appearances provided a useful chance to burnish my reputation back to a relatively clean shine, not unlike that on a much-loved suit of armour, but they had little or nothing to do with the actual making of photographs; when a motor-spares company approached us to ask if we'd care to provide a calendar we said yes immediately; we liked doing calendars. For most professional photographers calendars represent perhaps the gravest challenge and the greatest possibilities of all potential outlets for their work, save only the glossy, expensive and rather exclusive monograph. The reproduction is usually first-class and the pictures need to be equally good.

[ 165 ]

Any photograph that has the arrogant temerity to hang around for a minimum of at least twenty-eight days at a time has an obligation to be good, and ought to be excellent; I was game to give it a go.

A Kodak calendar to which I'd contributed had taken trees as its theme and I knew that the photographs I took (a tinsel Christmas tree in a forest of pines; a jigsaw-puzzle of monkey puzzle trees) had benefited from being so close to my heart. Filled with the false courage of sudden celebrity, I was ready for anything now, even motor-spares. I was being naive, of course; I should have realised that the last thing a motor-spares manufacturer wants to show to mechanics is motor-spares. When they told me it was nudes, I barely blinked at all.

As I told Leonora, rather grandly, a real photographer barely notices the objects that he finds in front of his lens; the real subject is the light itself. As she told me, with equal grandeur, if it was all right for Old Masters it was certainly all right for me. We were deluding each other, of course, but it seemed convincing enough at the time. I set out, in as workmanlike a way as possible, to assimilate the brief, found that there wasn't one really, and settled instead for a brief chat with (for once a not-undeserved title) the Art Director: Noel Myers.

My brief chat with Noel, a man for whom the term rough diamond was probably invented, lasted at least eight years and is by no means over yet; we discussed the difference between eroticism and smut, the precise definition of 'taste', and whether we were legs or chest men with an intensity that more than once spilled over into fisticuffs. (Noel's well-founded opinions on every aspect of the outward appearance of the female body are, infuriatingly, almost always correct but the aggressive strength with which he communicates his faith in his judgement all too often blinds one to the accuracy of his views.)

The first calendar we did together was shot in the depths of south-west France and looks, in retrospect, more than a little stylised – rightly so, in so far as it's a tribute to the wonderful props supplied by our stylist, Annie Calvas Blanchon. But wrongly so, in so far as it testifies to the almost studious air of detachment both Noel and I were so keen to adopt.

Terence Donovan, musing recently on the subject of nude photography, said that one of the biggest problems lay in answering the unspoken question: 'Why are these people here?' I thought at first he was referring to the huge crowds that seem to descend on any calendar shoot, even in the middle of the desert, but soon realised he had a much more subtle question in mind: what are all these naked woman doing on my wall? At a deeply simplistic level, the answer is obvious; the models were happy to be photographed in minimum clothing because, as one of them so immortally put it, 'It's better than doing knickers all week.' The idealised girls which the models stood in for, the malleable figures of fantasy for which their bared bodies provided a focus were, of course, a different matter entirely. The dream girls up on the wall said different things depending on how they were posed, and some of the things they said were less comfortable than others.

If the girl on the wall stares straight out of the frame, she's aggressive; if she come-hithers too much she looks cheap; if she pretends not to have noticed the camera she becomes, worst of all, uninvolved.

We tried all sorts of ways to arrive at an acceptable *modus vivendi* but it took us a while to get it right. In Carolina (old haunt of my forebear, where I was proud to be able to show the proprietor of 'The Lord Anson' a photograph of my latest triumph, the one-year-old Lord Anson) and in Kenya (where our make-up man tried to buy himself a Masai to take home for tea) we tried a mixture of all sorts and conditions and styles, whilst still posing the girls in unlikely positions in some subconscious attempt to show that they knew they were far from alone.

In Sicily we followed a far more aggressive strategy, vamping the whole thing up and throwing in large handfuls of decadence that began, however obliquely, to face up to the fact that, actually, these women had no clothes on; during our fifth year, with a return visit to France, the earnest detachment that we'd aspired to in our early days had settled in for real. We began to think of the girls as naked rather than nude, a fine distinction which somehow allowed us to let them sink back a little into the surrounding picture, taking equal billing with the landscape in which they were posed.

The regular members of the team who voyaged forth for fourteen days each year, Pedro, Chalky, Clayton Howard, Noel and Jackie Crier, our new stylist, were beginning to develop a heady sense of *cameraderie*, heightened by the shared experience of dealing simultaneously, year after year, with vicious mosquitos, unpredictable light levels, hostile locals and the resolute dogging of our footsteps by the film crew that had, somewhat mysteriously, materialised one day.

Spawning coffee-table books and television documentaries with casual abandon, the Unipart shoot was slowly becoming yet another institution, providing a focus for the unformed fantasies of thousands of people. Some of us found it easier to cope with this new-found fame than others, Clayton for one turning into a star with a suave insouciance that was miraculous to behold. The average model on the other hand, having emerged from Edgbaston and now heading for East Grinstead as fast as her high heels could carry her, found the sudden attention more than a little head-turning; we faced the additional burden of dealing with the unpredictable power of infant personalities flexing their slender muscles for the first time. Beauty, as I should have realised all along, can never be a substitute for wit, good humour or, dare one say it, loyalty (although, given the enormous sums of money that Fleet Street was apparently offering for a saucy story or two, one might in time forgive their proven determination to demonstrate that imaginations, too, can become unpleasantly over-developed).

Sebastian Keep, the seventh member of our plucky troop, who looks like a beach-bum turned white-hunter, fulfilled an almost undefinable but vitally important role in all the shoots, fixing things with an unhurried grace that made him, to my mind, wonderfully British. When, having decided on Spain for our sixth calendar, we realised that it was not the most liberated of countries in which to flaunt the flesh, it was Sebastian who suggested Ibiza (where, as someone pointed out, you can get arrested for putting clothes on).

Michael Pearson, on whose aptly-named yacht, *The Hedonist*, I had spent many a dissolute hour in times gone by, had settled in Ibiza after his marriage and very kindly took us on a tour of his house and invited us to take as many pictures as we liked before he departed on a brief duty visit to England.

Although the pictures weren't particularly stunning, we had a very enjoyable time, working extremely hard but still managing to squeeze in the odd moment in which to appreciate the local culture. (The average model preferred to stay and sunbathe with her sandwiches; one girl, offered a selection of guide books, said thank you, she'd read them when she got home.)

Leaving Michael's wife at their house one evening, anxious perhaps to show there was life in the old dog yet, I made an impressively speedy exit down the drive, turning promptly out of the gates to face a local driver coming straight at me like a bat out of hell. Swerving instinctively in precisely the wrong direction, I swung straight into a 120 m.p.h. impact.

Events are a little hazy thereafter. I remember the taste of blood in my mouth as I was bundled into a Citroën ambulance. I remember the sudden sight of a Spanish surgeon, wearing a rubber apron completely covered in blood. And I remember the look on the face of the hotel receptionist as, having discharged myself, I asked rather faintly for the keys of my room. I took two sleeping pills and slept like a baby; when I awoke it was to the sight of a man in a mackintosh taking photographs from the end of my bed. For the first time since my marriage, I wept.

And then, with nothing worse than a bad back, a few more lost teeth and a seat-belt-shaped bruise the width of my chest, I was back at home, in the rose garden at Shugborough, drinking in great heady wafts of scented air, utterly overwhelmed by the intense new experience of each passing moment. I resolved to take myself rather more seriously in future.

On our seventh Unipart shoot we pushed into the centre of Bali and discovered some astonishing landscapes. View after magnificent view unfolded one after the other as our minibus drove on through the mountains, transfixing me but leaving the average model beside me completely cold; she spent the entire journey with her nose in a paperback romance. We came back with some beautiful shots, using the distant semi-naked figures as elements in a series of almost orientally-balanced compositions, a deeply sensitive approach that was none too subtly sabotaged on the calender itself by the inclusion of additional steamy close-ups inserted at the foot of each page. (I simply cut off the lower six inches from every month; I lost the dates as well, of course, but who looks at a calendar for the date?)

Our eighth and last shoot scaled new heights of ambition for no better reason than we finally discovered the one place where we could be guaranteed to be almost alone: Death Valley at the peak of summer. Accompanied by Jilly Super-Trooper Cooper (whose presence alone made the entire trip a total delight), we drove over a hundred miles each day, worked from four in the morning till ten at night, sweated off pounds and produced the best calendar, indeed the best pictures, that I think I have ever taken.

The nudes were, at last, seen in their proper perspective, tiny flesh-coloured daubs dwarfed by the immense spaces around them, figures in a landscape at last.

One shot demanded a minuscule model poised perilously on the knife-edged summit of an immense sand dune twice as high as a house.

As she stood there in the far distance, glowing in the viewfinder like a garnet on a field of gold, I saw her stretch out her arm, open her hand and let drop a single sheet of brilliant pink Kleenex. As even Sebastian will confirm, there is no way to remove a piece of unwanted tissue from the middle of a vast expanse of pristine desert without leaving tracks. So we stood there, all of us, and watched the little pink relic blow first this way, then that way, up the dune and down the dune and up the dune again until finally, as the light faded, it scuttled out of the shot.

The model, who had to remain teetering in the sun whilst we waited, suffered more than most for her foolishness and was still, understandably, a little bit shaky at breakfast next morning. Preparing to sketch a perfunctory apology, I rather too brusquely asked her what was wrong.

'The trouble with you is,' she cried, 'you don't have to work with people like you.'

I wished, in a way, that she was right.

# [ 11 ]

Despite my persistent determination not to be type-cast as a specialist in any particular style of photography, one aspect of my career seems to have attracted more attention than most: my portrait photographs of the British Royal Family. All in all, I'm pleased that this should be so. 'Royal Photography' has provided me with the hardest, and most rewarding, pictures I've taken; I'm proud to have had the opportunity to make my own small mark alongside a long and highly honourable list that begins way back beyond Holbein, Hilliard and Winterhalter, goes on through people such as Baron, Beaton and Buckley, includes more recent names like Parkinson and Donovan and will, no doubt, go on growing for quite some time yet.

Ungrateful though it may sound, I nonetheless distrust the description 'Royal Photographer' which seems to be applied to me with monotonous regularity; in my opinion the only truly Royal Photographer was Lord Snowdon (whose influence, as anyone who watched Prince Charles' Investiture as Prince of Wales will know, has ranged far beyond mere photography).

'Royal Photographer' also implies, to my paranoid way of thinking, some kind of court appointment, like the Poet Laureate, and things simply don't work like that any more. As Albert Watson's work at Prince Andrew's wedding confirms, Buckingham Palace make a point of casting their net far and wide. Needless to say, one does not join this august company overnight; as with anything else there is a lengthy apprenticeship to be served and several tests to be passed along the way. My first picture of a Royal couple was a complete disaster.

When Encombe and I, having checked and double-checked every potential pitfall at least twice, set out for the Buckinghamshire home of the Duke and Duchess of Kent we were laden like pack mules; I was determined that nothing would go wrong.

When the hairdresser had finished with the Duchess' hair and the nanny had brought in the children, I arranged my four subjects into what I took to be a suitably formal pose and turned to Encombe for the camera. He refused to give it to me. I smiled nervously at our hosts, and tried again:

'Camera, please, Johnny.'

'Nnnh,' he said, shaking his head furiously.

*'Camera, please, Johnny!'*

'Nnnh!!' He leant across and whispered in my ear.

'We forgot to bring the film. . . .'

Brain somersaulting, I turned, rather slowly, towards where the Duke and Duchess stood frozen under the lights.

'My assistant is rather worried about your lights. . . ,' I began, and proceeded to spin a cock-and-bull story about the rapacious appetite of modern flash systems, before making a rapid exit in search, ostensibly, of a spare fuse. ('Don't move, I'll be right back.') There had to be a chemist somewhere close by.

There were many chemists, and all of them were closed; Wednesday is early-closing day in Iver, and in Uxbridge, and in Slough and, it seemed, throughout the whole Home Counties. The carnation-like bundle of wires brandished from his manhole by the G.P.O. engineer who directed me towards the last remaining possibility is etched on my mind still, as is the soapsud pattern being so carefully moved around the floor by the charlady I beheld there through the plate-glass window, a woman who only condescended to let me in after I'd mimicked a particularly convincing heart-attack on the pavement. I jumped across the counter, grabbed all the yellow boxes I could find, threw money in her generally astonished direction and hotfooted it back to Iver, where I found Encombe sitting on the floor, deeply dejected, whilst, at the other end of the room, the Duke and Duchess of Kent, the young Earl of St Andrews and the even younger Lady Helen Windsor stood, as instructed, in precisely the same positions as I had left them.

As we returned to London at the end of the session, I asked Johnny what kind of film we'd ended up with.

'Develop before October nineteen sixty-one,' he replied; the prints were more than a little misty.

Thanks to the great good grace of the Duke and Duchess (who, despite their ordeal, seemed only too happy to submit themselves to an identical one forty-eight hours later), we eventually did get some fairly satisfactory pictures; satisfactory but very stiff.

They could, in fact, almost be described as 'tweedy', a term which seems innocuous enough now but one which caused several small riots when used by Lord Altrincham in his notorious attack on the Royal Family's 'image', first published in a magazine article in 1957 (one enraged aristocrat threatened to shoot the blackguard).

Despite the uproar that greeted this piece of iconoclasm, Lord Altrincham's views, although less than delicately stated, seem not to have gone unheard; throughout the Sixties, in one of many communications revolutions that were happening at the time, a slow but subtle sea-change washed across the way in which the Royal Family presented itself in public.

The Queen, in particular (whose insistence on letting the television cameras into Westminster Abbey at the Coronation had prevailed despite the manifold objections of her advisers), seemed keen to allow the electronic eye even closer now, inviting it not just into Buckingham Palace but into virtually every other aspect of her life; Richard Cawston's *cinéma-verité* film, first shown in 1968, altered the public perception of the monarchy for ever, underlining the Royal Family's deep-seated professionalism and generating enormous sympathy for the heavy workload which they undertake on behalf of the nation. Royal portraiture was never to be the same again.

1966, the year in which I moved to Shugborough, Aubrey Walk and *Queen*, was also notable for one other event; it was the first time I took photographs inside the building whose peace I'd shattered so comprehensively with my clockwork revenge on Drummond. As I made my initial reconnaissance of the Throne Room at Buckingham Palace, where the pictures were to be taken, I was shadowed by a series of concerned-looking men; not (as I at first thought) private detectives but electricians, drafted in to make sure I didn't fuse the lights.

These silent supernumeraries proved useful as stand-ins when I took a couple of test shots, both of which, in truth, are rather more interesting than the real thing, a not entirely original image whose grandeur reflected the occasion it was intended to commemorate, the State Opening of Parliament. The Queen and Prince Philip, richly garbed, stand at one side of a huge doorway with Prince Charles, Princess Anne, Prince Andrew (in shorts) and Prince Edward (similarly dressed) on the other. Technically it is a perfectly adequate shot, with the huge open doorway giving the picture a nice sense of depth and allowing me to smuggle in some useful back-lighting from the room beyond. But it's not one of my favourite pictures; the pomp and circumstance of the occasion and the stateliness of the setting seem to have generated a sense of distance between the photographer and his subjects, none of whom (with the possible exception of Prince Edward) appear either happy or relaxed.

My next assignment was a distinct contrast, owing not a little to the new sense of informality that was suddenly abroad.

[ 175 ]

As Sir William Heseltine, then the Queen's Press Secretary, informed me over lunch at a club, a number of photographs were required for circulation throughout the year of the Silver Wedding Anniversary. The tone of the pictures was to be unposed, almost photo-journalistic in tone, and they were to be taken during the first leg of the forthcoming Royal Tour of the Far East. I was to join *Britannia* on its voyage to Mauritius, via the Seychelles, and then fly on with the Royal party to Kenya.

The prospect of sailing on the Royal Yacht (never, please, a ship) was daunting enough; the idea of taking photographs whilst doing so seemed even more alarming, but it was, in fact, not just a privilege but a genuine pleasure as well. The eye-dazzling sheen of the brasswork in *Britannia*'s engine-room reflected the same high polish with which everything about the tour was organised; the Royal progress proceeded like a well-oiled machine, with the hand of Sir Michael Charteris firmly on its metaphorical tiller. I crept around the outskirts doing my best not to interfere.

Avoiding flash whenever possible, I tried to catch the Queen and her entourage in as natural a light as possible and, after a few days, the click of my shutter became just another element in *Britannia*'s smoothly running routine.

A day or two before we docked in the Seychelles, we crossed the Equator, an occasion that was marked by the traditionally riotous ceremony of Crossing the Line. As one of the few novice sailors on board I, too, was dragged out of my cabin, escorted on deck, smeared with shaving-soap and plunged underwater, a procedure that caused a great deal of laughter from everybody present, not least from the Queen, who watched my plight leaning over the rail above the makeshift swimming-pool. She seemed to be completely unaware of the fact that I'd taken the basic precaution of packing my Nykonos, a small and, as the subsequent pictures prove, undeniably waterproof camera.

When, after we returned, I was invited to a weekend at Balmoral in order to take some more pictures in the series, the prospect, as with any other major commission, produced mixed feelings of alarm and elation, the latter emotion substantially tempered by the still raw memory of a recent shoot in Denmark. I flattered myself I'd done my bit to burnish the lustrous image of the English sporting gentleman by not only shooting, as we English say, not too badly but also by resisting the temptation to join my fellow guests in making what seemed like a tremendous fuss about what little success they had. During dinner, I realised my mistake when a major-domo entered and announced:

'I now vish to account the day's score. The King of the Hellenes: seventy-one pheasants. The Prince of Denmark: fifty-nine pheasants. . . .' Since nobody had told me otherwise, I'd neglected to let this man know my tally.

With the major-domo's final cry ('The Earl of Lichfield: No Pheasants At All!') ringing in my ears, I prepared myself for for Balmoral; they too, no doubt, would have their little ways.

Again, of course, the weekend (though run with characteristic efficiency) proved enjoyable and determinedly informal in tone; the Queen and Prince Philip, now joined by their children, seemed intent on simple relaxation, ministering at the loch-side barbeque, fishing for trout, walking the dogs (which included not only the ubiquitous corgis but also some impressive labradors) and generally being both gracious and professional enough to appear not to have noticed that one of their guests seemed to have a large glass and metal lump growing out of his right eye.

As I learnt long ago in the dear departed deb dance days, the secret of candid photography is to Be Prepared. I made discreet enquiries as to the usual daily routine at the Castle, discovered which doors, which rooms, which lochs and woods and burns were particular favourites, reconnoitred the terrain for hidden obstacles and opportunities, and kept an eye firmly open to every changing nuance of the light (which, in north-east Scotland in late summer can be even more unpredictable than the weather). That done, I settled back and did a very good impression of a man who was making it all up on the spot whilst hoping desperately that when the Decisive Moment came instinct would signal its arrival with a sufficiently loud alarm.

Not that anybody who stayed at Balmoral was allowed to sit still and merely observe; participation is all, particularly at the annual Ghillies Ball, where Madame Vacani's lessons finally came in very handy.

Riding, which also loomed large in the weekend's itinerary, has never been something at which I excel; I'd been a Foot Guard rather than a Horse Guard after all. Riding alongside the Queen, trying to make conversation and take photographs whilst keeping a tight grip on both reins and camera-bag was not exactly easy but when the time came for the shoot itself I was fairly confident that I had, or could see possibilities for, interesting pictures of each member of the Royal Family. There was only one exception: Prince Charles, whom I'd first photographed some years ago posing, in three successive shots, in the uniforms of the Army, the Navy and the Royal Air Force. Those pictures had been formal; now I needed something equally informal. Thinking photo-journalism, I attached a long lens and a motor-drive to the camera, determined to stretch the Decisive Moment, if it came at all, as far as it would go.

The weather is always nicer in happy memories but that second day was, I think, quite sensational. As we came down the hillside at the end of the morning, Prince Charles hung back to pick up his birds whilst the rest of us made our way down to the picnic lunch by the track-side. Just as we began to eat, Princess Margaret arrived with her children. Lady Sarah

Armstrong-Jones was devoted to Prince Charles and as they ran towards each other I slammed down my plate, picked up the camera and managed to squeeze the button just as the two of them met, arms flung wide, faces beaming. Seven of the shots I got, showing the two of them either too far apart or tangled together in a friendly blur, were useless; the third frame, which catches them decisively just at the right moment, is a particular favourite, freezing things just as they began to fall into place.

The motor-drive also proved useful when I was commissioned to produce an engagement photograph of Princess Anne and Captain Mark Phillips for a postage stamp commemorating their wedding. Despite the somewhat uneasy nature of my relationship with the Post Office over the years, their philatelic design team has, I believe, no equal in the world; the only problem with the precise brief they produced was that it called for the couple to pose with their heads closely enough together to fit within the frame. It's a pose that looks charming but is incredibly difficult to photograph; even the most lengthily married of couples finds it a strain to maintain that degree of intimate proximity for more than a minute or two at a time. Hence the motor-drive, and hence the stamp which, thanks to a great deal of professionalism on all sides, seems to work rather well. (It is always fun to photograph Princess Anne; one of my favourite pictures of her, taken to celebrate her thirtieth birthday, reveals the fact that it was taken in the pouring rain only on the uncropped, unofficial, version which shows, at the top left-hand corner of the frame, Clayton Howard's delicately manicured fingers clutching the handle of a protective umbrella.)

The final photograph of the remarkable baker's dozen that I shot during that enjoyable (if rather exhausting) weekend at Balmoral was a last-minute request, a posed group for use on a Christmas card. The photograph, showing the seven members of the Royal family back-lit by the late afternoon sun with the

Castle glowing behind them, is definitely informal, reflecting the relaxed air of that weekend; it is, on the other hand, by far the most formal shot in the series, given that it was the only one for which I actually had to ask anybody to pose.

Deciding, let alone striking, the right balance between the two extremes, the posed studio-type picture on the one hand and the candid snap on the other, is difficult at the best of times but with groups, particularly large groups, many of the decisions are made for you; the constraints of simply getting a picture where everybody has their eyes open, let alone anything else, virtually rules out any shooting from the hip. The manner in which the figures are arranged within the frame, however, can vary widely, as can the circumstances of the shoot.

Portraits of the entire Royal Family are relatively rare, not least because the times on which they are all gathered together in one place are few and far between, Christmas at Windsor Castle being a rare case in point. The genesis of the idea for the picture, Lord Snowdon's quiet enquiry as to whether I'd noticed that there was a Marx Brothers film on television that Boxing Day, was probably the high point of the operation; everything seemed to decline from there on.

The strategy seemed straightforward enough: set up a television set at the base of the tripod, space the twenty or so members of the Royal Family in a loosely-grouped arrangement around the room, and then simply press the shutter every time a joke hove over the horizon. Needless to say, it was not that simple.

The first problem was that the large drawing-room we had intended to use was unavailable, forcing us all into a smaller room further along the corridor. The second problem was that I then fused all the lights, and the third was the discovery that someone had rearranged the name cards we'd so carefully laid out around the room the night before.

Once we had everything sorted out, I reassured myself that problems always came in threes, and threes only, and climbed up my portable ladder to assume the position.

It proved far from easy to attract the attention of my audience away from Messrs Marx and towards the lens; I toyed, as ever, with the idea of falling off the ladder and decided that, under the circumstances, nobody would even notice. I did what I could, nonetheless, and took a great many photographs in a very short space of time, only to realise, problem number four, that the head of a faithful assistant appeared in each and every one, reflected in the ornate mirror above the fireplace.

Back at ground level at the end of the session, I took three overlapping shots of the group with a wide-angle lens, just to be on the safe side; luckily, as it turned out. Problems come, as someone said, not as single spies but in battalions; the three ground-level shots were the only ones that were even remotely usable. And so, through many long evenings at the studio, we pasted together endless permutations and combinations of the three originals, facing countless problems trying to overcome the distortion inherent in such a close use of a wide lens. For the final picture, which received wide distribution, we had to resort to drastic cosmetic surgery, cutting off at least five heads and replacing them with substitutes from other shots.

Despite this radical and faintly republican solution, the final photograph still seems to work, not least because of the way in which the people in it are dotted around the room in what looks like an almost random manner. Other groups, particularly wedding groups, and especially Royal wedding groups, proved rather less easy to construct.

I was in Sicily, doing my best to be decadent for Unipart, when Felicity rang me with her regular up-date on the studio news, mentioning in passing that she'd slotted in a fairly major booking for a Wednesday in late July. The precise date meant nothing to me at the time but, several hours later, it began to ring a small bell.

It was only when I got back to the studio that I saw the news in the papers: I'd been selected to take the official photographs of the wedding of Prince Charles and Lady Diana Spencer, a prospect which, put like that, sounded so daunting that I promptly did my best to forget all about it.

Time passed and, when it became clear that there was nothing I could do to delay the fateful moment, I finally faced up to the horrific nature of the challenge before me. The first, and probably biggest, problem I foresaw was the whole question of timing; I'd be lucky if I got even as much as half an hour in which to take the pictures, and half an hour meant precisely that; one minute either way and I'd run the risk of incurring delays in the whole of the day's subsequent schedule. Furthermore, unlike the Duke and Duchess of Kent, we wouldn't simply be able to rearrange the entire event if anything went wrong. So: check, double check and go on doing so until the photographs were safely out of the labs and on their way to Camera Press for distribution.

Second problem: the press (and, indeed, television and, indeed, virtually every communication medium in the world) would need everything I could get and more, not only on colour transparency, but also on colour negative and on black and white. So: lock four cameras onto one joint mount and get them to fire simultaneously, ideally with Hasselblad's own patented device. Or, if that proves to be unavailable (in China as it turned out), get somebody to knock one up. Or, when that doesn't work either, think the whole idea through again. And again. And again.

Third, and hopefully last, problem, as I discovered when we went to do our first recce: we were not alone. Two gentlemen in mackintosh would also be taking photographs at my side. So:

[ 182 ]

er, don't know, think of something, anything to gain an unfair advantage.

Fourth problem, and the greatest of all: how to arrange so many people, organised within the strict limits of both wedding protocol and Royal precedence? Although I didn't know what on earth the dress would be like, it seemed safe to assume that it would be fairly spectacular, and that the bridesmaids and pages would be similarly dressed. So: a tight central group, focused probably on the bouquet, taking in bride, bridesmaids, pages and, slightly to one side, the bridegroom. Either side, a long line of bright frocks, emphasised by, behind them, a solid phalanx of senior males, most of them no doubt in dark uniforms which would point up the colours of the ladies in front whilst toning down the less tightly serried ranks behind.

In principle it sounded fine but, in practice, a difference of mere inches in height between one guest and another could make or break the picture. So: I sighed, mapped out a model of the Throne Room steps in cardboard off-cuts, and settled down with a box of matches, a sharp knife and a comprehensive list of the heights of each of the fifty-five people involved.

On the morning of 29 July 1981 the short drive round the corner from our flat in Eaton Square to the back gate at Buckingham Palace took ten minutes and seemed to last an age; the only light relief was the sight of Chalky and Dawkins (who was substituting for an otherwise-engaged Pedro) trying to look as if they always wore morning suits when working.

The first thing we did once we'd unpacked the gear in the empty Throne Room was to switch on a television set, just in time to catch the bride arriving at St Paul's, wearing a magnificent dress with a train that was a full twenty-five feet long. Not a problem, I told myself; we'd fit it all in somehow. The next thing I checked was the inner balcony of the Throne Room, overlooking the courtyard, where I wanted to try and take a few

[ 183 ]

quick natural-light pictures at the very end of the session. The white sheet I'd asked for as a background was ready and waiting, pressed, with predictable efficiency, into a series of knife-edge creases, each of which would show up only too well in the finished photographs. Not a problem I told myself; we'd just have to retouch them out afterwards.

As the newly wedded couple returned down the Mall towards us, the sound of the crowd, which had ebbed and flowed beneath the window all the while, grew from a rumble into a roar that broke, finally, into an explosive cataract of sound as the procession came through the archway beneath us; it was the most delightful, and the most terrifying, noise I ever hope to hear.

I rushed to take a few candid snaps from the inner balcony, attempting without success to smooth the sheet in passing, and then ducked back in again to the Throne Room where I expected to see the constituent parts of the wedding group already beginning to gather. The room was empty. Fifth problem: the traditional balcony appearance had been re-scheduled. The wave, which was greeted with rapturous applause, was followed, to even greater applause, by the kiss, a kiss that, captured by the photographers on the wedding cake outside the gates, promptly echoed round the world before I'd shot a single frame.

And then, suddenly, the room was filling with a chattering throng of crowned heads and sundry relations, all of them clustering around the numbered chart we'd pinned up on the wall to inform them where to stand (an idea brought back from Luxembourg by Prince Philip, and a very welcome way of reducing the already large scope for milling chaos).

To my total astonishment, the placement worked out exactly (with the sole exception of Princess Grace of Monaco whom we had to ask to stand on a telephone book; not a problem, we always carry a spare).

I now had sixteen minutes in which to do the job. I took a few shots, dutifully echoed by the mackintosh on either side of me, but the assembled guests, thoroughly convivial, were by now chattering happily amongst themselves whilst the precious minutes ticked away; time for the Acme Thunderer. The piercing blast of the referee's whistle proved gratifyingly effective.

The crowned heads of Europe, their ears still ringing, peeled away as planned to leave the middle group, the immediate family. As I went forward to adjust a bridesmaid's dress, Prince Philip informed me of problem number six: one of our lights wasn't working.

There were three possible causes with three possible solutions, each of them more complicated than the last. The first idea worked first time. Perhaps my luck was changing.

Now we were left with the final group, the bride, the groom and their supporters, all of whom we quickly rearranged around the train (which turned out, rather cleverly, to be completely detachable).

As the expectation of lunch grew almost tangible in the air, my stiff collar turned rapidly to the consistency of damp blotting paper, and I realised that there was still one problem outstanding; the mackintosh men who were still shadowing my every move. There seemed little point in the three of us turning out identical pictures. Without even knowing why I did it, but with some vague memory of a Western I'd seen as a child, I did my best to imitate the noise of a camera shutter with my tongue.

It worked; the press photographers promptly zipped off another brace of shots. I now had a one-shot lead. But what was I to do with it? Remembering, *Nil Desperandum*, the family motto, I plugged on gamely to the end of the roll, the Prince and Princess of Wales visibly wilting as we began to run out of time.

Finally, as the press photographers came to the end of their last roll of film, I straightened up. 'Thank you, everybody,' I said to the wedding party. 'You can relax now,' and they did, falling into a confused, very human and informal huddle on the floor. Without conscious thought, I squeezed the shutter release on the last frame of film, capturing the very moment when everything fitted into place, as we English say, rather well.

## CODA

Much of my precious spare time lately seems to be spent looking out of windows, particularly at Shugborough where long perspectives have always been something of a speciality. The west front of the house, the side without the colonnade, the gravel, or the stern stone steps, has always seemed the quieter, more domesticated of the two and the back-lit view from there towards the end of a summer afternoon is pleasantly appropriate in scale: the rose garden and the mown terraces leading down to the river and the meadow beyond, framed by a protective wall of distant trees.

I catch myself sometimes, with an irritation that is all the more familiar for being only faint, detaching myself from every-thing the landscape means to me to see it only as another problem waiting to be solved. How would I photograph it?

The roses, and the lawns, would definitely have their place, as must the river itself, though to stop the subtle reflected movement of the light upon the water, even for a moment, would be an injustice. Beyond the farther bank, the field has thistles (perhaps I could find a way to hide the thistles) and a herd of White-Park cattle, many of them possibly descended from the patient animals I puzzled over thirty years ago. In the back-ground, lost as yet against the bosky outline of their larger, older neighbours, stand the trees I've planted, the fifty-two varieties of oak I've nurtured as my own small contribution to the look of the estate.

You can just make out the *Quercus oglethorpensis* there, grown from some tiny acorns I pilfered from the White House lawn several years ago. The spindly little sapling will grow sturdy soon enough; by the time of Tom's majority it should provide, with luck, just enough scant shade to shelter him or either of his sisters, Rose and Eloise, when they need a place to think, or watch, or simply sit and read a work of fiction.

Even if I managed to freeze the river, hide the thistles, capture a little of the splendour of the roses and the glory of the oaks, would it be an honest picture? Honest, possibly; truthful, well . . . professional photographers reserve the right to tamper with the truth a little here and there, in pursuit of private visions. Reality's rather relative at the best of times; all we can offer is one aspect at a time, one angle, one story from amongst a thousand.

This book, of course, is also a convenient fiction, framed, composed, selected to produce the desired image. Some episodes, (like the sudden death of my mother, the eventual move from Aubrey Walk or most painful of all, the end of my marriage) are too personal to be dealt with here; they, like the thistles, must remain, as far as I'm concerned, outside the frame (the men in mackintoshes will tell a tale or two if you encourage them; they're in the story-telling business now).

Other moments, easier to remember, have no doubt been delicately retouched here and there as time's gone by; I like to keep things neat. Above all the need for contrast has lightened some characters (most notably mine own, which seems to show no trace of impatience, anger, greed or laziness) and blackened others (I owe Jocelyn, for instance, far more than any tribute here can even touch upon); some people seem to have slipped

[ 187 ]

the net entirely (like Eddie Lim, my hyperactive partner in London's Tai-Pan restaurant).

Truth or fiction, the story has to end somewhere; the shutter finger writes, and having writ, moves on. The future remains an unfocused mist of possibility; there is still time for me to emigrate, remarry, make my maiden speech in the House of Lords, drag down the family name in final shame, succeed, fail, muddle through, speed up, slow down, or, more than likely, simply settle for the mixture as before, and keep on going, filling the unforgiving minute with sixty seconds' worth of distance run. If past events are anything to go by, the story is far from over yet; we shall just have to see how the picture develops.

# INDEX

N